# LIFE AT THE TOP

Mark Hodkinson is a freelance writer, working mainly for *The Times*. He has previously contributed to *When Saturday Comes* and has written biographies on Marianne Faithfull and Prince, among others. He was born in Manchester but now lives with his partner and their one-year-old son in West Yorkshire. He has been a full-time writer since 1989 after earlier working as a journalist for several weekly and daily newspapers.

# LIFE AT THE TOP

## A brief taste
## of the big-time for
## Barnsley Football Club

## Mark Hodkinson

Photographs by
Justin Slee

*Queen Anne Press*

Queen Anne Press
is a division of Lennard Associates
Mackerye End, Harpenden
Hertfordshire, AL5 5DR

First published in Great Britain in 1998

A CIP catalogue record for this book
is available from the British Library

ISBN 1 85291 602 8

Cover design by Design2Print
(with acknowledgement to the original design
for *Room at the Top* by Penguin Books)

Printed and bound in Great Britain by
Clays Ltd, St Ives plc

# CONTENTS

# FOREWORD
## by
## Barry Hines

At the beginning of the 1997-98 season when Barnsley were promoted to the Premiership for the first time in their history, I visited an exhibition of football memorabilia at the Cooper Art Gallery in Barnsley. In one of the rooms, surrounded by old photographs of players, posters and exhibits in glass cases, three youths dressed in Barnsley replica shirts were sitting on a sofa watching a video of edited highlights of Barnsley's promotion season. Every time Barnsley scored they cheered and punched the air, and when the video ended, they sang, 'It's Just Like Watching Brazil'; the unofficial Barnsley Football Club anthem. I was touched by their pride and loyalty for at last, following years of hardship after the miners' strike and wholesale pit closures, the town and its football club had something to shout about.

I felt the same way reading Mark Hodkinson's perceptive account of Barnsley's short lived residency amongst the football elite. Through a combination of analysis and interviews he builds up an entertaining picture of both football club and the hard pressed community which supports it. I enjoyed this book enormously. 'The boy done well,' as they say in football circles.

BARNSLEY F.C.
COMING SOON
TO OAKWELL
THE CARLING
PREMIER LEAGUE

# INTRODUCTION

'Life At The Top' was the name of a column that appeared each Saturday in *The Times* throughout the 1997-98 football season. The idea came from the two men at the helm of the newspaper's sports coverage, David Chappell and Keith Blackmore. Other publications had included pieces about Barnsley, but they recognised the significance of Barnsley's promotion to the Premiership and that it would make a fascinating on-going story.

My brief was fairly loose: I was to write it as I found it. They trusted implicitly that I would find character, humour, and colour, though they probably did not legislate for the odd spat along the way. Still, football is life, and life is often blunt and to-the-point.

Throughout the season I maintained the vain hope that readers who were not necessarily Barnsley supporters, or indeed football followers, would enjoy the column. The subject matter is incidental when the prose is rich, the energy irresistible, or something like.

Barnsley were good hosts, though not the much-fabled 'perfect'. The club is not fond of flies on the wall and they are swatted without a second thought. They are suspicious of outsiders and slow to trust. When I asked Danny Wilson if I could travel on the team coach, for example, his eyes turned to stone, and so did I. 'No,' he said, the words hardly necessary.

Other clubs, Sunderland most famously (with the television documentary, *Premier Passions*), are considered enlightened because of their open door policy, but Barnsley leave you waiting in the corridor, and not just metaphorically. They do it their way, which means with a fair degree of privacy and caution. This is not to say that the club is not staffed by friendly, good-natured people, because it is. They are also genuine 'football' people. They know the game, love it, talk it, and there is no affectation. Pretentiousness is more or less extinct in Barnsley.

Repeatedly, I was told that if the columns were gathered together they would form a succinct record of Barnsley's flirtation with the big time. A book would also provide an opportunity to give a greater insight into the life of a football club. Sometimes, the process of gathering information is more interesting and revealing than the information itself.

The articles were written contemporaneously and are reprinted here much as they appeared in the newspaper. One or two swear words have been put back into the copy and I have tightened up the odd sloppy phrase or two. On occasion, it was sometimes gracious to temper thoughts and opinions to stay on good terms with club officials; football clubs and their supporters are notoriously sensitive. I have added more background to some of the articles, and tried to 'speak' more directly, especially now I have diplomatic immunity.

I did not attend every Barnsley match. While I wanted to shadow the club, it had to be at a few paces. Familiarity, in journalism at least, breeds obsequious and banal copy. Where I did attend a game and report on it, the report is included. In places, this has led to a spot of repetition but it provides a bulletin from the heart of the action, out on the pitch.

A great many people have lent their support to this book. Firstly, I would like to thank the sportsdesk at *The Times*, Keith Blackmore in particular, for believing in the project, and myself, and allowing me to shape the columns with very little interference, but a great deal of encouragement and enthusiasm. The sub-editing was generally sensitive and thoughtful, despite one or two hilarious exceptions. In one infamous issue, we had John Dennis with 'bricks in his seat' rather than 'bricks at his feet'. Either way, the reader got the point. Mark Herbert, Peter Dixon, Richard Whitehead and Tim Rice were particularly supportive.

Once the book was commissioned, *The Times* permitted a smooth passage into the new format. David Chappell, sports editor, made favourable noises to management; Mike Murphy and Gertrude Erbach sorted out the technicalities; and George Brock, managing editor, gave his permission without recourse to the brow-knitting that often accompanies such a decision.

Mal Peachey deserves thanks for trying to place the project

(then in a different guise) with various publishers. Unfortunately, his efforts were in vain, but he set a trail which led from Mick Middles to Adrian Stephenson, a man willing to trust a hunch and finalise a deal within a matter of days.

Barry Hines kindly agreed to write the Foreword and, on more than one occasion, offered a telling perspective on the enigma that is Barnsley. On a personal level, it was a joy to meet a literary hero and find that the energy and compassion of his work was a mirror of his personality.

The staff on the town's excellent weekly paper, the *Barnsley Chronicle*, were particularly helpful, especially Andrew and Keith Lodge. The irrepressible Benny Hill provided many insights, proof-read the manuscript, and was not shy of offering the odd opinion or 10. Andrew Ward supplied some valuable phone numbers and Malcolm Moyes sent me several well-written articles and fanzines. Every Barnsley player I approached was, without exception, obliging and candid. The office staff and boot-room team were also highly accommodating.

The Barnsley supporters were kind and helpful, and it was a pleasure to share their company. In the places where I have been critical of their behaviour, it is of the unruly minority, and not the thousands of loyal, decent Barnsley fans. I hope these good people will not find themselves apologists for the few who besmirch Barnsley's good name. Every club has its share of thugs, Barnsley - probably because of the novelty value of their situation - collected a few more than most in their season of glory.

All the people interviewed gave their time free and did not impose any conditions. As I set up camp in hotels, service stations, cafés, pubs, living rooms, board rooms, kitchens, or wherever, I often thought how fortunate I was that my interviewees were so guileless and keen to talk. It would have been a long, laborious season otherwise.

Finally, my girlfriend Paula was advisor, proof-reader and just about everything else. Over the years, she has become used to losing me to Rochdale FC and dealt with the additional blow of my adopting another football club with commendable understanding.

# CHAPTER ONE
## Loyal Fan, Ticket Wanted

*Saturday 5 April 1997*

**Barnsley 0 Birmingham City 1**

Barnsley's defeat was only their second in the previous 13
league matches. They remained on course for promotion from
Division One of the Nationwide League, nevertheless.

Bolton Wanderers secured promotion to the Premiership with a
2-1 victory against Queens Park Rangers.

———————

LOFTY AMBITIONS REALISED ON BOLTON'S BIG DAY
*(match report, The Times, Monday 7 April 1997)*

**Bolton Wanderers 2 Queens Park Rangers 1**

Rooted to the bottom of the Premiership, 21 defeats already
endured, relegation inevitable, Bolton Wanderers played
Chelsea exactly one year ago today. Ruud Gullit jogged lazily
onto the pitch to warm up before the kick-off. As he
approached the Burnden Terrace, the stand containing
Bolton's most vociferous and partisan supporters, he was
greeted by a spontaneous round of applause. Surprised, he
tossed back his dreadlocks, raised his arm and acknowledged
their generosity of spirit.

This was the England of the myth: a country of gentlemen
where hearts were warm and sportsmanship intact, even after a
season of wretched defeats. Magnanimity in defeat is an
admirable quality and it is right and proper that it should be
rewarded. A year on, a 2-1 victory against Queens Park Rangers
has secured Bolton's promotion back to the Premiership. They
need just two points from their last five matches to become
champions. It is a testimony to Bolton's magnificent season that
they should celebrate promotion with a month of the campaign
remaining. They have lost just four times in 41 league games
and have scored three or more goals on 13 occasions. The

promotion party was everything, the match a mere incidental, which was appropriate for a nondescript game.

Television cameras roamed the club car park in search of a flat cap with a quote, and the giant urn of tea in the press room was empty an hour before the kick-off. As usual, the master of ceremonies was the club's mascot, Lofty the Lion. Sassy and spry, he has few equals and his agents may face a busy summer deflecting offers from other clubs requiring his flamboyant touch. Watching a man pretending to be a lion pretending to be Freddie Mercury has a remarkably warming effect on a chilly, windy day in the North West. Queens Park Rangers, who might themselves still secure a play-off place, did not succumb to the mood of levity and promptly scored an excellent goal. Morrow collected the ball a good distance from Bolton's penalty area and, within the blink of an eye, it was in the net.

Once more the crowd was privy to Bolton's famous philanthropy. 'A lovely goal by QPR, scored by No 6, Morrow,' said the match announcer. There was enthusiasm in his voice, as if seeing this piece of skill – by a member of the visiting team – had actually given him pleasure. Bolton equalised before half-time when Blake's shot was parried and Fairclough stabbed home from close range. The party was back on and Lofty was already dancing on the touchline ready for his interval histrionics. The win, and promotion, were confirmed when McGinlay deflected a shot by Thompson beyond Sommer.

At the final whistle, not a single Bolton supporter ran on to the pitch and this allowed the players and fans to celebrate unfettered. Thompson, sporting a T-shirt reading 'We're up and we know we are', danced wildly with Blake, while Taggart careered into Lofty and wrestled him to the ground. This was not a reticent, self-conscious affair, it was 11 men gone mad, not to mention the substitutes, management team, and the squad players paraded in their suits.

The sun stubbornly refused to shine. A thick buttress of cloud remained steadfast above the floodlights and the wind whistled through the old stadium. Anything else would have been unbecoming: Bolton had to win promotion in Bolton weather.

Lofty joined in the lap of honour and staggered as he took pretend sips from bottles of champagne. 'I've never seen a lion drunk before,' said the announcer, before revealing that Manchester United had lost to Derby County. 'Oh, our cup spilleth over,' he added quickly.

Queens Park Rangers played their part and adopted the sportsmanship of their hosts. Colin Todd, the Bolton manager, was congratulated by every Rangers player as they left the pitch and a group of about 40 of their supporters remained on the terraces to witness the lap of honour. They applauded warmly as the Bolton players passed. At such moments, the world can seem a better place. Afterwards, it seemed churlish to ask, but someone had to, and Todd already had an answer prepared. Did he feel that Bolton were better equipped to survive in the Premiership than they had been last time? 'Let's enjoy the moment,' Todd replied. 'We'll talk about that later.' It was said without a hint of rancour. Bolton truly, madly, deeply enjoyed their moment. Tomorrow can wait.

---

*Saturday 19 April 1997*

### Crystal Palace 1 Barnsley 1

A penalty by Neil Thompson meant Barnsley had secured seven points from a possible nine in the three matches since losing at home to Birmingham City. Promotion was within sight.

After the game, Steve Coppell, the Crystal Palace manager, began a theme that was to continue for some time: 'Barnsley are a good side,' he said. 'They haven't bought success nor kicked their way past teams. They have no big-name stars, and everything they have achieved has been born out of hard work, team spirit and commitment. Barnsley are the team the whole division feels deserve to go up because they have done it in the right way.'

---

# LOYAL FAN, TICKET WANTED

*Saturday 26 April 1997*

**Barnsley 2 Bradford City 0**

A 2-0 win against Bradford City sealed Barnsley's promotion to the Premiership. It was the first time in the club's 110-year history that it had reached football's top division. Paul Wilkinson and Clint Marcelle were the scorers.

---

BARNSLEY SAVOURS CHAMPAGNE MOMENT
*(match report, The Times, Monday 28 April 1997)*

They were still dancing in the stands, their feet tapping out a broken rhythm that reverberated above the dressing-room area. These places, the inner sanctums of football clubs, are a world of their own. Ladies push tea trolleys past young men in tracksuits; directors in thick overcoats head to their private bar; the smell of liniment meanders through corridors. On Saturday, at Oakwell, this pungent aroma was sweetened by that of champagne. Every other person who walked by carried a bottle and a smile to match its sweetness. Finally, Danny Wilson, the Barnsley manager, appeared. Resplendent in a blazer and tie, he leaned against the polished wood panelling. Above him was a notice: 'Football boots must not be worn beyond this point.'

Wilson has honest brown eyes and a confident but genial manner. His team, cut from the rough stone of free-transfer players, local boys made good and the odd import, had just secured promotion to the Premiership, but, surrounded by notebooks, he seemed unaware of the magnitude of the moment. He talked of team spirit and loyalty, camaraderie and wisdom. There was a dignity about his politeness and patience as the world thundered in joy around him. 'They have been very good to me at this club,' he said. 'We believed that we could go up and there has been a good spirit all season.'

It may take some time, perhaps years, before Wilson can

articulate the significance of Barnsley's achievement. By virtue of assembling a successful team in a provincial Yorkshire town, he has become the champion of the underdog. The heart of every supporter of every small-town club will have skipped a beat. Oakwell was busy two hours before kick-off. Supporters without tickets held up pieces of paper on which they had written messages like, 'Loyal fan, ticket wanted'. The drizzle caused the ink to wash across the paper. The Bradford City team coach arrived and, benevolent to the end, a Barnsley supporter shouted to the players as they alighted: 'Tha's going down, tha knows.'

Dickie Bird, the former Test umpire and a Barnsley follower for 56 years, gave the first of scores of interviews beneath a huge umbrella. Several supporters milled around in sombreros, wearing painted-on, drooping moustaches – Barnsley's style of play has been compared to Brazil's, hence the South American theme. 'It's just like watching Brazil,' the supporters sing. The recorded version features a rap segment over which the phrase 'Barnsley Football Club' is repeated with odd menace. It seemed more than vaguely incongruous, perhaps like Barnsley playing Manchester United or Arsenal in the Premiership.

The players, much to their credit, were remarkably unconcerned by the commotion and provided a fine game. Wilkinson headed bravely past Davison in the 21st minute and thereafter the game flowed from end to end, with plenty of scoring opportunities. Marcelle, a substitute, guaranteed the win, and promotion, after a mazy run through the Bradford defence with three minutes remaining. Stewards and police tried desperately to keep supporters off the pitch, but their ranks were broken soon after the final whistle.

When a team has waited 110 years to make the country's top division, there is inevitably going to be some party. They sang in the rain, danced on the dugouts and demanded that the players returned. Stewards helped the players to clamber through the stands and they duly waved their fists and champagne bottles to the crowd. They threw down shinpads and socks as souvenirs, and Eaden even parted company with his shorts and had to negotiate a return to the dressing-room past team-mates keen to hurl his jockstrap to the masses. The press box was partially invaded and journalists were unable to phone over copy in the pandemonium as handsets were swirled above heads.

In the streets around the ground, drivers beeped their horns and flags were waved at passers-by. Radio phone-ins were jammed with callers congratulating Barnsley. From Brighton to Berwick-upon-Tweed, the goodwill flowed munificently towards South Yorkshire. As the streets cleared slowly and the drizzle continued, it seemed odd that football, a mere game after all, could galvanise such warmth and sense of community. There was also a gnawing sense of anticlimax – to be at this epicentre of happiness and not be a Barnsley devotee. Their supporters had waited 110 years: how long will it take for our own dreams to come true?

---

Few neutrals, if any, were privy to the promotion parties of both Bolton and Barnsley. It was fascinating to witness the different responses to success. At Bolton there was an absolute respect for the sanctity of the pitch and the players on it, a clear demarcation. Fans were content to clap and cheer and witness the horse-play of their heroes.

The celebrations at Barnsley were out of control, a reckless, chaotic carnival. It was a new experience for these supporters, and this largely accounted for the bloody-minded unruliness of it all. Thousands spilled on to the pitch and though the majority did so through sheer exuberance, others were involved in scuffles with stewards and police. There were continual altercations between police and fans who climbed on top of the dug-outs. Amid the smiles and jigs and tears of joy were these snapshots of anger. It seemed peevish at the time to mention this undercurrent of recklessness and no comment was made in the press. It was a day for the good people of Barnsley, the loyal and the decent.

It was my first visit to Oakwell. I arrived early and parked in the car park given over to away supporters, a grassy slope at the end of Grove Street. The radio was already singing Barnsley's song, chronicling their years in the wilderness, and their sudden, unexpected rise to eminence. 'Aye, I never thought we would ever have a chance of going up, like,' said a middle-aged man, caught by a radio microphone somewhere between the market and Woolworths. Everyone interviewed spoke of their incredulity, as if promotion was something to which they had no right, somehow above their station. 'I still think they'll blow it at the last minute. You watch 'em, they'll lose agin Bradford today,' said one unbeliever.

Bradford City were embroiled in a relegation battle and their supporters were focused on the solemn, nervy business of survival. I walked alongside them as they made their way to the ground. They spoke quietly, too anxious to raise a cheer, their throats parched. These huddles of claret and amber were soon lost among the mosaic of red and white.

Dickie Bird held court on the pavement. His restless Yorkshire twitter cut through the drizzle and people stopped to watch. It seemed strange that this famous voice, so often heard on television and radio, should just ring out across the street, the street on which we were walking.

Michael Parkinson was also at the game, and his presence brought a prickly comment from Benny Hill, a retired sports journalist who was to become a great ally during my season with Barnsley. 'It must have been a big match because Michael Parkinson arrived to write about it!' wrote Hill in the Supporters' Club magazine, *High Hopes*. He added: 'So the star writers were given a row of seats behind the directors' box – apart from Parkinson, that is, who, for some unaccountable reason got a seat in the box.'

Barnsley, I learned later, had a strange relationship with its two celebrities, Parkinson and Bird. 'Between them they have about as much personality as a dehydrated worm,' wrote one letter-writer to the *Barnsley Chronicle*. The week afterwards, there were enthusiastic letters of support, but the mocking continued in the Barnsley fanzine, *Better Red Than Dead*. It announced a bogus grand charity auction, offering as Lot 1: 'Michael Parkinson's entire collection of match tickets collected over an entire lifetime of supporting the Reds. The collection consists of one item: Barnsley v Bradford City, 26 April 1997. Minimum bid £10.'

The press contingent was so large that many of us were placed among the supporters in the West Stand. We were granted a superb view of the game, and were privileged to sense the Bovril-hot intensity of emotions, but it was impossible not to feel uneasy. I have been asked many times what it was like to be part of such an historic day. It was like calling at a stranger's house where a celebration is under way for a wedding or christening. Out of a sense of duty, they open their front door and provide the best seat in the house. Their happiness and warmth serve only to distil the visitor's solitude, and, by the end of the afternoon, it becomes oppressive and the journey home a sweet relief.

I was positioned close to the directors' box and, throughout the game, I witnessed a bizarre cameo. A Barnsley fan, stripped to the waist, was turning continually towards the directors. Head shaved, purple-faced, he mouthed 'thank you' to them, and stretched out his arms in supplication. He then turned back to the game and vented his fury, screaming obscenities at the Bradford players. The directors pretended not to notice; there was no other way to deal with this confounding mixture of passion, aggression and gratitude.

At the final whistle, the cameras lingered on the excitable fans who had raced on to the pitch. Up in the stands, where the majority remained, it was a time of reflection. They remembered their first-ever visit to Oakwell, the friends and family they had gone along with down the years, some of them now dead. At that moment, everything - the painful, ignominious defeats; the cold, wet, miserable afternoons at Hartlepool and Scunthorpe; the years of well-meant but hurtful teasing – felt worthwhile, as if it had contributed to something magnificent.

Afterwards, *Better Red Than Dead* carried unaccredited supporters' testimonies under the heading of 'What Did You Do On The Glorious 26th Dad?' These were the people to whom it mattered most:

'I don't remember seeing Clint pop in the second goal, just the crowd's reaction and the utter relief and joy, the tears in Joanne's eyes, getting on the pitch and dropping on my knees to kiss the ground and getting a gob full of muck, the unbelievable atmosphere, and finally, the expression of shock on my dad's face after 48 years of sufferance.'

'The Reds going up is two fingers to the fat cats, like crashing the posh knobs' cheese and wine gathering with a party-sized can of Watney's Red Barrel and spraying it in their faces.'

'I have been watching Barnsley since 1959, but what can I say about Saturday? I have not experienced such intense emotions since the birth of my kids. Saturday was the culmination of a long journey for me. Can anything top that? The day was made even more complete by the attitude of the Bradford fans, clapping us at the end in a most generous fashion. Also, let's not forget John Dennis's contribution. Barnsley through and through. His dad would be proud.'

'At the final whistle, tears were wept in joy, but also for those parents and grandparents who had walked down Oakwell Lane and Grove Street only dreaming about that moment and who never got to see the likes of which were seen that day.'

For my part, I was thinking of my own footballing legacy, the years spent at Rochdale's Spotland ground, the apparent futility of it all. In my 23 years as a supporter, during which time I had missed no more than five home matches (before starting work for *The Times* in January 1996), I had never seen them escape the bottom division and our highest league position had been eighth in the 1991-92 season.

Throughout Barnsley's Premiership season, everyone connected with the club would empathise warmly whenever I mentioned my support for Rochdale: 'Is that pub still there, on the corner? I think it's near a cemetery.' 'Are the pies still really good?' they would ask. Repeatedly, they would mention the last time the two teams had met in the league, on a sunny day in April 1979. A victory that day would have all but guaranteed Barnsley promotion from the old Fourth Division but Rochdale won 3-0. It had been a rare win in a season of habitual defeats.

As the celebrations took place all around me, I realised starkly that my own team would never reach the Premiership. It was too late. Barnsley's ascent had begun two decades earlier. There was now too much ground to make up. The drawbridge had been slammed shut.

Barnsley's success was supposed to inspire lower league clubs, but paradoxically it also killed the myth. It had been nearly 20 years since Barnsley had last met Rochdale, outside of cup competitions. The football world had changed completely, there was no longer any comparison. All that seemed to remain at the place Barnsley once stood were perpetual 1-1 draws with Hartlepool and endless afternoons of thick-set men booting the ball randomly from one end of the field to the other.

The promising young players who were once happy to hitch themselves up to a professional football club, any professional club, were now signed by Premiership teams after being spotted in the playground. The academies set up by the top clubs, including Barnsley, ensured a steady flow of talent, but it meant that the pool had been drained of talent for all the other clubs without the finance to set up their own hot-house academies. Likewise, seasoned professionals in the twilight of their career were increasingly choosing to retire gracefully, rather than risk a broken leg or two among the tree-cutters of lower league football.

Barnsley fans hold a great deal of sentiment for clubs like Rochdale and their ilk, but much of this camaraderie is based on nostalgia. They are fortunate to be out of touch with this cul-de-sac of British football, where the mediocre take on the modest in a quarter-full (at best) all-seater stadium, and the country cares so much it is served-up 20 seconds of highlights on television at 1 am on Tuesday morning.

All the same, true supporters know that discarding your football club is like discarding a member of your family. The hurt and the humiliation might be intense and frequent, but the love is unconditional. I might outline a damning case of the futility of supporting Rochdale, but the team has a magnetic pull, beyond all rational thought. When the ball hits the net and Robbie Painter (our best striker) submits himself to a huddle of fans behind the goal in celebration, I want to shout, scream, cry, laugh, and levitate, all at once. So, at Spotland I shall remain, happy in the sadness of it all.

---

*Friday 2 May 1997*

The headline in the *Barnsley Chronicle* was designed purely to sum up the euphoria in the town, but it inadvertently started a panic. 'We're Up! Now Ticket Rush Begins' cried its front page. Ticket rush? Most supporters were still drunk on promotion champagne, and had not stopped to think that they might miss out on their club's legendary season.

---

*Wednesday 14 May 1997*

Danny Wilson was voted Manager of the Year by his fellow managers, forcing Alex Ferguson, the Manchester United manager, into runner-up spot. 'I am very flattered and very privileged to be honoured in this way,' said Wilson.

---

*Friday 16 May 1997*

There was now genuine panic in the town that there would not be enough season tickets to meet demand. It was compounded by an unusual policy whereby existing season-ticket holders had the right to buy two season tickets in addition to one for themselves. It was designed as a reward for their loyalty, a gesture of thanks; they would be able to share the experience of Barnsley in the Premiership with two others from their network of family and friends.

Unfortunately, the policy was patently flawed and caused a pall of animosity to hang over Oakwell at a time when happiness should have prevailed. In hindsight, it was difficult not to see the operation as a rather canny – others might call it cynical – attempt by the club to draw in maximum capital for minimum effort.

Along with most supporters outside the Premiership, Barnsley fans, in the main, subscribed to the tradition of simply turning up on Saturdays and paying at the turnstile. Even during their promotion season, the number of season-ticket holders formed less than 25 per cent of the total attendance at each game. As a measure of loyalty, the season-ticket system was inappropriate, since thousands without them still attended game after game, home and away.

Obviously, it was only fair that existing season-ticket holders should have first right to Premiership season tickets, and this was never disputed, but their extra two tickets were to be distributed at their discretion. While many were passed on to keen supporters, whether they be old fans enticed back, or people willing to give up Saturday jobs now their team was in the Premiership, others fell into the hands of casual supporters, 'glory-hunters' as they were dubbed.

In the worst scenarios, loyal supporters were fraught with worry that they might miss out on their team's glorious season, while the person at the bar next to them, who had never mentioned their love of Barnsley before, was safe in the knowledge that his uncle (who he saw twice a year) had guaranteed him a season ticket. 'As in the strike of 1984, it has turned friend against friend and father against son,' wrote P Woodhall to the *Barnsley Chronicle*. 'Why has the club which prides itself on integrity betrayed its true supporters in favour of those who merely wish to see established Premiership clubs play?' asked Frank Beevers of Mexborough.

In the club's defence, the allocation of tickets was a massive and unprecedented administrative task, and one which would almost inevitably draw criticism. The club's logic was that it would be (almost) as easy to sell each person three tickets as it would one, so the procedure would be simpler to process. Barnsley, though, has a populace of great sensitivity, to whom loyalty is a beacon. They saw the ticket policy as grossly unfair. The indifferent and the capricious already had their tickets, while the devoted fan – who had never felt the need to become a season-ticket holder – was left in an agitated state hoping the 'Sold Out' sign would not be placed across the window as he reached the counter.

*Saturday 17 May 1997*

Thousands of supporters found themselves eligible for season tickets after all the priority sales had been made. They began queueing on Friday night, some arriving with deck-chairs and barbecue sets. By early morning there were thousands packed on to the car park, and the mood of bonhomie changed drastically.

Despite employing extra staff, club officials struggled to process the applications because of the sheer volume. They decided it would be impossible to administer more than 800 and handed fans numbered tickets which showed their place in the queue, so they could return at a later time. Others were asked to put their application information into envelopes for processing throughout the week.

Understandably, people who had queued for up to 10 hours were furious to leave the scene without a season ticket in their hand. 'Michael Spinks' management of season-ticket sales [Spinks was the club's general manager/secretary] has proved to be the mother of all administrative cock-ups,' wrote one supporter to the *Barnsley Chronicle*. *Better Red Than Dead* carried a tirade against the club's perceived bungling, concluding unsympathetically: 'The whole thing was a lot of shit in the organisation department.'

# LOYAL FAN, TICKET WANTED

## *Thursday 22 May 1997*

The club had taken to issuing almost daily news bulletins assuring supporters that hundreds of tickets remained. 'There is no need to panic,' promised Michael Spinks.

---

## *Friday 30 May 1997*

True to its word, the club did have enough season tickets for everyone. Approximately 1,500 tickets were put on general sale, all for the West Stand, the only part of the ground for home supporters which had not been renovated. Most of these were sold, although there were still a further 100 seats available which were sold throughout the season on a match-by-match basis.

The only unfortunate legacy of the furore was that some supporters found themselves housed in parts of the stadium where they did not wish to be, while others, who probably did not care a great deal anyway, were in coveted seats, most notably in the Ora Stand, which was the traditional base for the most committed supporters.

The more cynical fans had predicted a dissipation of passion with the introduction of these indifferent special guests. They warned that there would be a 'dead spot' every few seats or so, where the nouveau supporter was sitting, silent and deep in thought, trying to remember to which end Barnsley were kicking. The atmosphere, in the event, was unaffected and there was no noticeable reduction of intensity. Oakwell was rarely anything but white-hot.

The club scored valuable popularity votes by selling season tickets at an affordable price. There was no attempt to increase them significantly and 'cash-in' on Barnsley's new status. In fact, the tickets were the cheapest in the Premiership. The most expensive tickets were £250 for the upper tier of the East Stand, while it cost £200 for a seat in the Ora Stand. In comparison, Chelsea charged £887 for a seat in the middle of Stamford

Bridge's East Stand. Even the fanzine was prepared to offer a sprig of gratitude: 'Congratulations to the club for their pricing policy on season tickets: it is much appreciated.'

---

### Wednesday 11 June 1997

While other newspapers had run a handful of features on Barnsley, *The Times* decided to 'adopt' the club for the season. I was commissioned to write a weekly dispatch on this club which had attracted such unprecedented national interest.

I sent a letter to Danny Wilson, asking to 'share Barnsley's season from touching distance'. He replied that, since the media interest in Barnsley had been so phenomenal, he did not think it would be possible.

---

### Friday 11 July 1997

Another letter was sent to Oakwell, this time to Wilson and the club chairman, John Dennis. My tone was more jocular, I implied that *The Times* would go ahead regardless, and it might be better all round if I was not left shivering on the club car park.

---

### Tuesday 29 July 1997

Danny Wilson replied: 'On this occasion I will give authorisation for your column in the Times.' The word 'authorisation', used in this context, struck me as unusual.

---

*July 1997*

Danny Wilson augmented his squad with a handful of signings, drawn from around the globe. 'Foreign players represent better value for money,' he explained. Eric Tinkler, a South Africa international with 30 caps, joined from Cagliari in Italy for £650,000. Cagliari had just been relegated from Serie A. Ales Krizan, a defender and Slovenia international, joined for £450,000 from Maribor Tartrnec, while Lars Leese, a tall German goalkeeper, signed for £250,000. The former Bayern Leverkuesen player had spent the end of the previous season on loan to Barnsley.

The most expensive newcomer was Georgi Hristov, at £1.5 million from Partizan Belgrade. The 19-year-old striker had come to notice after scoring the winning goal for Macedonia in a World Cup qualifying match against the Republic of Ireland. Despite his relative youth, Hristov had already played 14 times for his country. Within a few weeks of signing, his name was the most popular on the back of replica shirts sold at the club's shops. John Hendrie was second, and Arjan de Zeeuw third.

Before the summer, the club's highest transfer fee had been £250,000, paid on two occasions, to Middlesbrough for John Hendrie and to Darlington for Matty Appleby.

During the close season, friendlies were played against Tiverton and Yeovil in the West Country and against local teams, Chesterfield, Rotherham and Doncaster. A week before the start of the season, Santos, the legendary Brazilian side, visited Oakwell and a crowd of more than 11,000 saw them beat Barnsley 3-0.

Ladbrokes made Barnsley 1,000-1 to win the championship. Supporters were surprised to learn that Crystal Palace were made 250-1, even though they had struggled to make the Premiership via the play-offs.

---

*Sunday 27 July 1997*

An Open Day at Oakwell attracted a crowd thought to be in excess of 10,000.

Players struggled to make their way from their cars to the ground, such was the demand for autographs.

----

*Tuesday 5 August 1997*

Darren Barnard was Wilson's sole domestic signing when he joined Barnsley from Bristol City for £750,000. He had scored 14 goals in the previous season from his left wing-back position. He had played for England as a schoolboy but during the course of the season made his full début for Wales against Jamaica. He was born in Rintein, Germany, where his father served as a soldier, so was eligible to play for any of the home countries.

----

TOWN SQUINTS IN HISTORY'S GLARE
*(The Times, Saturday 9 August 1997)*

The sun is shining on Barnsley. Liam Gallagher's familiar brick dust and glue whine beckons from a record shop. Young girls, 14 and a-courtin', gather at the entrance to the market precinct. In Peel Square, the Tommy Wallocks pub has a loose assembly of lunch-time drinkers resting against its portal. This heat. It is all they talk about. 'But it's too humid, isn't it? Not like you get abroad,' one old boy says to another, his canvas shopping bag by his feet as he sits on a bench outside Marks & Spencer.

The world ambles by, all loose-limbed and languid. At first, the crowd of shoppers is a blur. There is then a trickle of recognition, like a familiar face spotted in a group photograph. One red shirt passes, then, a few seconds later, another. On each is the white rose of Yorkshire and the unusual word, Ora. These are the shirts of Barnsley FC (Ora is the club's main sponsor), and it could be a trick of the imagination, but the wearers seem to have a spring in their step, a smile on their face. Barnsley FC, after 110 years, have finally reached the highest strata of English football. At 3 pm today they will play West Ham United at their Oakwell ground in the Premiership. It will be an all-singing, all-dancing occasion with more than an hour's worth of pre-match entertainment; plenty of time for the *Match of the Day* cameras to focus on a tear wiped, a face painted. When a club has waited this long – precisely 5,714 weeks – it is clearly not going to be one of those restrained affairs where no-one dares start the first dance. Overstatement is a journalist's accomplice, but we are fast running out of words to relate the magnitude of their achievement. A heavy snowstorm is a white hell, every car crash horrific, so the impassioned response to Barnsley's success is said to be at 'fever pitch'. It is actually beyond this. It is at the cold-bucket-of-water-and-a-nurse-on-standby stage.

At the beginning of last season, Barnsley had 2,500 season-ticket holders. It now has 16,500. The club sold eight times as many replica shirts during the first weekend they went on sale than in the whole of last season. Some fans even camped overnight outside the club shop (sorry, Reds Superstore) so they could be the first on Barnsley's streets in the new shirts. Cynics have predicted that the fervour will be short-lived. Such a suggestion is anathema in the town, a load of Tommy Wallocks, so to speak.

The media interest is phenomenal. It sees a parable, David and Goliath, and romance, and a certain sentimentality. Danny Wilson has tried to remain stolid amid the clamour. This is a man who, as a player, turned out for eight different clubs in nearly 800 league matches. He wants to hear the crunch of shinpads, see shirts drenched in sweat. In short, he wants the hubbub to subside. The people of Barnsley are enjoying the attention, though a certain wariness and scepticism prevails. They feel a media that has come in search of romance had previously shown apathy, or worse, suggested that the fauna was solely whippet, ferret or pigeon and the flora non-existent, apart from the odd weed among the cobblestones.

It is, in fact, typically provincial England, an Anytown UK. It has dual carriageways and industrial estates, car parks and Kwik-Fits, and beyond the housing estates there is open countryside stretching to Leeds, Sheffield and Manchester. Aside from the sporting commotion, the heart of the town has beat much the same as it ever did during the summer of 1997. It was the last summer for the actor Brian Glover, an ex-pupil of Barnsley Grammar School, and also for Stan Bradder, a 79-year-old former miner. Stan died in a chair at his home, and before his body was discovered, thieves broke in and stole some of his possessions. The following night, as Stan remained slumped, they repeated the robbery, ripping open his mattress looking for money; there is evil in every Anytown UK, sometimes to the power of two.

The news pages of *The Barnsley Chronicle* have also related the absurd. In June, the town was swamped by the smell of rotten eggs. Environmental Health staff found high levels of sulphur dioxide in the air and averred that it had blown over from Doncaster; Yorkshire towns are fond of the odd spat, whether it be over sport or noxious fumes. Cameras, microphones and notebooks will sweep through Oakwell today, but by Monday the weekend's newspapers will have faded in the sun and Barnsley, a nation's beloved underdog, will start to feel like sepia-tinged news. Thereafter, the poetry will give way to the mud, blood, sweat and slog of a season in professional football. Wilson is ready, Barnsley is ready, a season awaits.

---

*Saturday 9 August 1997*

### Barnsley 1 West Ham United 2

Barnsley took the lead through Neil Redfearn but John Hartson and Frank Lampard Jr scored to record a 2-1 win for the visitors. Darren Barnard had to read the names on the back of his team-mates' shirts to identify them.

# LOYAL FAN, TICKET WANTED

## Wilson Keeps Faith With Homespun Ideals
*(match report, The Times, Monday 11 August 1997)*

The sandwiches were already turning brittle and starting to curl in the overheated press-room. Danny Wilson took two steps into the stuffy heat and made a shrewd decision: 'Come on, let's do it outside.' The sun shone into his eyes and he had to squint, but few beads of sweat crossed his forehead. He looked a man at ease, even under an unforgiving sun, even in defeat. 'I'm glad this game is out of the way and we can get away from all the hype. Hopefully, we can settle down again now,' he said.

Defeat had not made him despondent. He had the same look of relief as the groom enjoying a crafty cigarette after the nervy formality of the wedding ceremony. The cheerful assurance of last season has patently remained, despite his club's new status. 'We've got to get to the pace of the Premier. The fairy-tale stuff didn't happen today,' he said. Locally, there had been talk of a possible flying start to the season, with three of the first four games at home and the one away match at Crystal Palace, a team, like Barnsley, just promoted.

Since Barnsley secured promotion, Wilson has spent more time in front of cameras and microphones than with his players. Or perhaps it just seems that way. He has told the same jokes, relayed the same anecdotes, and the magnitude of his team's first game had been reinforced constantly. A game of football is a simple affair, as ephemeral as a British summer, but the build-up to Barnsley's season – and specifically this match at Oakwell on Saturday – had been tortuously overplayed. The rhythm of expectation had been played repeatedly on a booming, slack drum and we were left with a headache born from underdog overload.

Wilson, commendably, opened the season with approximately the same team that clinched promotion. Only Tinkler and Barnard supplemented a winning combination, so signings from Macedonia, Slovenia and Germany were left to pass around the sun-cream on the substitutes' bench. Obviously, when so much has been invested in a game of football, the absolute logic is that it will descend into bathos and it did. The streets thronged with life, balloons were sent skywards, the crowd sang gloriously, the match was pretty awful.

It started well enough. Wilkinson met a deep cross and steered it towards Redfearn, who instinctively redirected it across Miklosko. It was fitting that Redfearn, the club captain and a Yorkshireman, should score the first Barnsley goal in the top division. Barnsley have two fine proponents of a long-forgotten art in Bullock and Hendrie. They are both expert dribblers, able to caress the ball with their instep and move gracefully past players of greater physical stature. In the kick-and-rush heat of a summer afternoon, their artistry was pleasing, though not properly rewarded.

The visiting team showed nothing but bruising endeavour in the first half, but found a rhythm after the interval. A hopeful cross was met bravely by Hartson and he lifted it into the Barnsley net. Watson, who had seemed nervous in goal, had left his line and had to watch it sail over his head and outstretched arms. West Ham had two Frank Lampards on the bench. Frank Lampard Jr, son of the former West Ham defender who is now assistant manager, was sent on to add pep to an already industrious midfield. He played a simple pass at the halfway line and then moved stealthily through the Barnsley defence to meet a cross from Lazaridis. Lampard scuffed the ball, but this served to place it cruelly beyond the diving Watson.

Harry Redknapp, the West Ham manager, said afterwards that a tactical switch at half-time had guaranteed the victory. 'We overloaded the midfield after the break and took control of the game. Barnsley worked hard. No one will come here and have an easy game, I can promise them that,' he said. Wilson agreed that his young goalkeeper was to blame for the first West Ham goal. 'In this division, you can't give anyone half a chance, because they will take it. The keeper made the one mistake and the ball was in the back of the net,' he said. Al fresco press conferences will remain collectors' items at Barnsley this season, and Wilson now has to work long hours on the training ground to ensure that home defeats are of the same scarceness.

---

Typically, pundits used the game as a barometer of Barnsley's season. Much was written about their alleged naiveté, but, in truth, it was a close game between two well-matched teams. West Ham, marked down as potential relegation candidates before the season began, enjoyed a creditable season, rarely falling below mid-table.

A handful of West Ham fans were attacked after the game when they made their way back to the visitors' car park. It was noticeable that the police presence was increased markedly by the next home match.

---

*Tuesday 12 August 1997*

**Crystal Palace 0 Barnsley 1**

A powerful shot by Neil Redfearn earned Barnsley a 1-0 win at Crystal Palace. The victory lifted Barnsley to eighth in the first published league tables of the 1997-98 season. It would remain their highest position of the season.

---

*Wednesday 13 August 1997*

A crowd of more than 1,500 attended Oakwell to see the reserves beat Rochdale 5-0. The reserves enjoyed a good season, winning promotion to Division Two of the Pontins League.

---

FALLING VICTIM TO FIRST-DAY NERVES
*(The Times, Saturday 16 August, 1997)*

Television regularly serves up dramas on the theme of apocalypse. The bomb is about to drop, heads fall into hands, misanthropists prowl the streets; the whole world has gone Roswell. Barnsley town centre had this sense of eeriness last Saturday afternoon. At Oakwell, just a mile away, there was colour and life, but the centre could have been brushed by tumbleweed.

Marks & Spencer was deathly quiet, like a Sunday staff-training day. The only customers were a handful of old ladies cruising the aisles in search of corn plasters and tins of butter beans; nothing, not even a measly Armageddon, could deter these ladies. Peter Gibbons, the manager of Boots, confirmed that trade had been affected by Barnsley's début in the Premiership. He had no complaints though, three of the Barnsley players had recently popped in for a pedicure. 'They carried themselves off well,' he said, almost with a hint of surprise, as if he believed every footballer learned etiquette from Carlton Palmer. (*Carlton Palmer was involved in a court case where he was accused of assaulting a young woman in a Yorkshire night-club.*)

The only signs of life were young men outside pubs, glasses of beer in hand, high on anticipation. Many were wearing their replica Barnsley shirts, but others had taken them off to reveal chicken soup skin, going tomato in the sun. It was not so long ago when a match at Oakwell would take place almost unnoticed by residents living in the red-brick houses around the ground. On Saturday, they waved from deckchairs as the crowd filtered through.

BBC trucks had commandeered part of the car park and cameras roamed in search of a talkative Tyke. The queues for match programmes stretched into the side streets and new businesses had appeared overnight – badge selling, burger selling, Barnsley selling. The pre-match entertainment was a tad choreographed, but, on such a momentous day, nothing was left to chance. The crowd sang, rather unoriginally, 'You'll Never Walk Alone', and hundreds of balloons were released from beneath a giant canopy. It appeared as if every Barnsley supporter was wearing a team shirt and, clearly inspired, the team were beating West Ham United 1-0 after just nine minutes. The visitors went on to win 2-1 and the sense of anti-climax was stifling. There were even echoes of a statement made nearly 100 years ago when Barnsley were first elected to the Football League. A committee member had muttered in 1898 that the team 'might not uphold the dignity of the club in such surroundings'.

A victory at Crystal Palace on Tuesday, granting Barnsley their first Premiership points, has helped assuage these feelings of inferiority. Barnsley is a club waking up to its new status. It aspires to the hospitality age, but there remains an anachronistic, home-spun charm. A phone call to the ground, for example, is answered by a real person, rather than the spurious politeness of an automated switchboard. The toilets at the rear of the West Stand are open to the elements and visiting supporters are housed in a stand without a roof. Meanwhile, the other two stands, the Ora and the East, are magnificent and the entrance to the ground features a vertical curved window set in brick, giving it a distinctly ecclesiastical touch. It is this nearly-there, half-finished quality that makes Oakwell unique in the top division.

At the end of last season, a handful of reporters were housed among the fans, but the press box has been expanded this term to deal with the deluge. There are plenty of seats, although the aisles between them suggest that measurements were taken using Dennis Wise as the average size, when Kevin Pressman might have been more appropriate. The programme is a colourful and detailed affair, but here Barnsley again reveals its mixture of pragmatism and ambition. There are assiduously researched articles running alongside 'Tommy Tyke Sez'. Tommy wears a cloth cap, scarf and bemused expression and talks to the world in a treacle-thick South Yorkshire accent. He has a special message to the cynics: 'We're gooin' ter surprise a few fowk, an slap egg all o'er t'feces o't scoffers.' A club big enough to laugh at itself might well be big enough to survive in the Premiership.

---

## A Fan Who Really Makes Headlines
*(The Times, Saturday 23 August 1997)*

Life on a local newspaper is fraught. There is invariably a reader at the reception desk grumbling that his daughter has been mistakenly married to the best man, or that the golden wedding couple had their honeymoon in Scarborough, not Cleethorpes. They hate Cleethorpes. It always rains when they go there, the shops are awful, they had their first row in Cleethorpes.

There are very few free lunches, both metaphorically and literally, for the diligent scribes who amass column inches under the watchful, sensitive eye of their own community. So, when the man from *The Times* calls at the *Barnsley Chronicle* promising the wondrous delights of chicken in a basket et al, one might expect a 'Yes please, make mine a turkey in a hamper' response. Think again, for this is Barnsley, home of the pragmatist. 'No, thanks, I always bring sandwiches on Mondays,' is the response from Keith Lodge, the paper's sports editor.

Lodge has spent 37 years at the *Chronicle* and has covered Barnsley Football Club throughout this time, from the old Fourth Division to the Premiership, Eric Winstanley to Georgi Hristov, Hartlepool to Arsenal. He hoped originally to pull on a Barnsley shirt, a goalkeeper's, but after training with the club as a youth he decided instead to write about it and became a reporter on his home-town newspaper. Rather like the club, Lodge has suddenly found himself a conspicuous figure since he is Barnsley FC's most trusted and reliable messenger. He has missed just four matches, home and away, in the past 20 years and his expert knowledge is mined shamelessly by his peers in the press box.

The *Chronicle* is based in a sunny office in Church Street, a pleasant stroll away from the impressive town hall. Lodge has not yet had time to eat his sandwiches, but kindly assents to another interview about his beloved Barnsley. He is dressed conservatively – neat shirt, plain tie, pen in pocket. He wears metal-rimmed glasses and, appropriately enough, a Michael Parkinson haircut. He is friendly, but wary. He has not been best-pleased by the way that Barnsley has been portrayed over the past few weeks. His report on their opening game, against West Ham United, was an unequivocal broadside to his contemporaries from the national press. He bemoans the caricature of the Barnsley fan 'clog-clomping down the cobbled streets'. 'It's of no relevance, all that stuff,' he said. 'We've had an awful lot of coverage and I think a good deal of it has been patronising.'

Many have pondered on the source of Barnsley's success, though few have the benefit of Lodge's antecedence. He remembers watching them when attendances were sometimes below 2,000. 'It's down to Danny Wilson and the tremendous support he has had from the board,' he said. 'He has worked his socks off for the club and I think his man-management is superb. I like Danny. He is an informal chap. You can always knock on his door.'

Lodge has worked long hours filling pages of news about Barnsley's fortunes, helped by his son Andrew, who is also a sports reporter on the paper, and his sister Sheila, a part-time employee. The paper has rightly recognised that these days are halcyon and it sings the town's delight on every page. Amid this rarefied Premiership air, the *Chronicle*'s sub-editors have dreamt some fanciful dreams, hence bizarre headlines such as 'How Psycho Found God' and 'Fancy That: A Turbo-pigeon'.

When the fixtures were announced earlier in the summer, Lodge was aware that he would have to miss the game that fell on 25 October. As a member of the North Gawber choir, he was due to perform at the Royal Albert Hall. 'And guess what? It's only the day when we're due to play Manchester United at Old Trafford,' laughed Lodge. The choir will now be one voice down on the day. It was a game he could not miss. There will be other unmissable games, starting with the visit of Chelsea tomorrow. Fancy that: a turbo-powered season.

---

LIFE AT THE TOP

*Sunday 24 August 1997*

## Barnsley 0 Chelsea 6

Chelsea arrived at Oakwell with the cameras from Sky TV, effectively making it the match of the weekend. The subtext was simple: the Kings Road meets the red-brick side-streets of Barnsley; the household names meet the unknowns. Barnsley were outclassed and lost 6-0. They had no answer to the fluidity of Chelsea's movement. Gianluca Vialli, who became Chelsea's player-manager later in the season, scored four goals. The others were scored by Gustave Poyet and Dan Petrescu.

----

*Wednesday 27 August 1997*

## Barnsley 2 Bolton Wanderers 1

New signings Eric Tinkler and Georgi Hristov scored in a 2-1 home win against Bolton Wanderers. Peter Beardsley pulled one back for Bolton.

A few days after the game, Barnsley received a letter from Edward Waddington, a Bolton supporter, making a desperate plea: 'Such was my thrill at Beardsley's début goal, my toupee became unclipped from its moorings at the back of my head. I think it might have blown to the back of the Spion Kop. Have any of your cleaners come up with a strawberry blond-coloured appendage?' No trace of it was ever found.

----

HRISTOV RESTORES BARNSLEY MORALE
*(match report, The Times, Thursday 28 August 1997)*

Team spirit is much mythologised in sport but can rarely be quantified. At Oakwell last night Barnsley went some way to providing the benchmark by which it can be measured. On Sunday they were trounced 6-0 by a slick Chelsea team and the bookmakers were instantly revising their odds on the Yorkshire team suffering instant relegation. At 5-1 on, it had the appearance of another ignominious scoreline. Against Bolton, their old adversaries last season, Barnsley rallied magnificently and served up a thrilling, end-to-end match in the process. There was no evidence of fear in their boots as they returned to their crafted passing game with chances falling repeatedly to Hristov and Hendrie.

'The response tonight was exactly as I had expected it to be,' said Danny Wilson. 'They were hurt on Sunday and the only way forward was to bounce back with a win.' The only disappointment on a night of passionate, flowing football was a head injury sustained by David Watson, Barnsley's young goalkeeper. He suffered concussion and will not be able to play again for up to three weeks.

Barnsley started with the spring back in their step and their Yorkshire-patented brand of total football bewildered Bolton for the first half hour. Their studied but lively approach-play was rewarded when an unmarked Tinkler headed firmly past Branagan from a Redfearn free kick. Barnsley's infamous benevolence was manifest once again when the defence failed to repel a rare attacking move by Bolton. Peter Beardsley stepped graciously amid the chaos and chipped the ball over Watson. Just two minutes into the second half, Barnsley restored the lead with a splendid goal by Hristov. The Macedonian, making his full début, rose majestically to meet a measured cross from Barnard. The match swung enigmatically in the balance thereafter with chances created at both ends. The best fell to Hendrie who stumbled into Branagan when he was put through clear on goal. Bolton pressed forward searching for an equaliser but found Barnsley determined to secure their second win in the Premiership.

Colin Todd, the Bolton manager, said afterwards that his team needed to adopt a 'meaner' attitude. 'We do not have the guile at times to make that extra pass that can make the difference. We need to be meaner.' Barnsley, in contrast, showed a great deal of meanness. They tackled hard, chased valiantly and handled the ball with a great deal more care than they had on Sunday. Three days is a long time in football.

---

HURRICANE VIALLI: THE AFTERMATH
*(The Times, Saturday 30 August 1997)*

Solace does not exist in a 6-0 home defeat. It is a deathly scoreline, one that even non-football fans will recognise as surreal. 'Didn't their goalkeeper turn up?' they will ask. 'Did someone lace their cups of tea at half-time?'

Danny Wilson steadfastly faced the press minutes after his team had been annihilated by Chelsea at Oakwell last Sunday. Football folk tend to talk in euphemisms, but there was only one left for Wilson, so he used it: 'It's not the end of the world.' Make no mistake, 5.50 pm on Sunday would have felt like Armageddon for Wilson. This was, after all, the Barnsley nightmare: their team savagely outplayed, made to look slow, thoughtless and, much worse, awkwardly out of place.

'They toyed with us,' admitted Wilson. It received extra emphasis because it was played on a Sunday and broadcast live by Sky television. It was like inviting the family around for Sunday dinner and forgetting to switch on the oven, an indignity turned into a catastrophe. It was 6-0 everywhere you looked: Vialli's retracted foot, the net bulging, the clenched fist, red shirts and red faces slumped to the ground, again and again. The hushed tones with which the score was relayed made it seem that a team so neglectful as to concede six goals would be relegated on the spot. This is largely because Barnsley and relegation have been synonymous since before the season began. When Barnsley lose, it is viewed as a precursor to demotion, but for anyone else a defeat is an aberration, a blip in their form.

It is almost as if Barnsley's presence in the Premiership is seen as a massive stroke of good fortune. In fact, they are in the top division because, over the course of last season, they were consistently a better team than all but one of their peers (Bolton

Wanderers) in the First Division of the Nationwide League. It might seem peevish to mention, but on Sunday evening Barnsley were still higher in the league than, among others, Liverpool, Sheffield Wednesday and Aston Villa. Also, many commentators failed to point out that a 6-0 defeat brings about precisely the same points tally as a 1-0 deficit. The real forfeit is measured in the psychological damage it can inflict and this appears to have been fairly minimal.

On Wednesday, Eric Winstanley, the Barnsley first-team coach, shared some of the media duties with Wilson. A former player at Oakwell, he was not known for his delicacy of tackle and his prose is similarly brusque. Typically, death was mentioned again. 'Either you lie down and die or you bounce back,' he told reporters before the match with Bolton.

Barnsley won 2-1 and played with the joyous abandon of a team that had merely read about someone being humiliated 6-0 rather than suffered it themselves. On this occasion, Sky was elsewhere, so the result did not have the same resonance. This will not cause them to weep into their beer in Barnsley because there have been a few too many cameras roaming the streets of late. It has even become difficult to find a gaggle of excitable youngsters willing to jump around manically over the shoulder of a hapless interviewee. The exceptional has quickly become the commonplace. While the media has been intrusive and intense, it has also been surprisingly respectful in its portrayal of the club and town.

There has, of course, been mention of the traditional stereotype – the whippets, the pigeons, the cobbled streets – but in an affectionate way. Some observers have yelled that the town has been patronised, though this is a fairly ill-defined charge. In any area of life, sport or otherwise, a complimentary remark is often interpreted as patronising these days. Barnsley, on the whole, has done extremely well by the media. It is a town that has its own culture, which is unashamedly parochial. One lead story in the local papers this week was about Harry Potter, a former baker who has decided to spend his retirement racing pigeons. 'I've gone from being a pie widow to a pigeon widow,' said his wife, Elaine. Pies, pigeons: this is post-modernism, Barnsley style.

---

*Saturday 30 August 1997*

## Derby County 1 Barnsley 0

Stefano Eranio scored a twice-taken penalty to inflict Barnsley's third defeat in five matches. Lars Leese made his full début, while Ashley Ward played his last match for Derby.

CHAPTER TWO

Bleeding Hopes and Dreams

*Thursday 4 September 1997*

Ashley Ward signed for Barnsley just five days after playing against them for Derby County. He brought Barnsley's spending to almost £5 million, which meant the club had spent more in a two-month period than it had in its entire previous history.

Barnsley were Ward's eighth club after spells at Manchester City, Wrexham (loan), Leicester City, Blackpool (loan), Crewe Alexandra, Norwich City and, finally, Derby County. His first transfer fee when he left Manchester City for Leicester was £80,000. He cost Barnsley £1.2 million, with a clause that Barnsley would pay a further £250,000 if they avoided relegation from the Premiership.

Ward proved to be Wilson's best signing of the season. Strong and willing, he supplied the focal point that had been missing from the attack. 'His workrate is fantastic and he has got goals in him as well. It is arguably the best signing I've made – possibly will ever make,' said Wilson. Ward returned the compliment: 'I like the way Barnsley play. Their style suits me.'

---

GHOSTS THAT HAUNT GAME'S FALL GUYS
*(The Times, Saturday 13 September 1997)*

The moaning starts just minutes after the kick-off. 'Play the bugger to feet, will you?' shouts an old boy in a fawn anorak, his voice almost lost in the wind. Down on the pitch, the play remains fractured and almost wilfully negligent. The old boy turns in his seat, looking for another soul to share a glance of resigned empathy.

The stands at Boundary Park, home of Oldham Athletic, are sparsely populated, so the grumbling echoes all around. These are the ghosts of Premierships past, where the wailing never stops and a glorious yesterday taps persistently on the shoulder. Just four seasons ago, Oldham Athletic were in the top division. Almost every seat was taken as the likes of Manchester United,

Arsenal and Liverpool visited a ground that is one of the highest above sea level in England. It really did feel like heaven was within touching distance.

The town, with its terraced houses, disused mills, perpetual rain, and pop groups with names like Wonky Alice, suddenly had glamour by association. A staunch following of about 4,500 supporters tripled and cars were festooned with club stickers as everyone claimed part-ownership of their home-town team. This same fervour has engulfed Barnsley since they secured their place in the Premiership.

Success not only brings Manchester United to a football club, it also brings queues, parking problems, ticket shortages, street vendors and thousands of new converts, usually in such numbers to significantly change the atmosphere within a ground. 'It all suddenly became very strange,' said Pete Mason, editor of the Oldham fanzine, *Beyond the Boundary*. 'It got so that you knew the people who stood near you, but there was then all these new people. I would be selling the fanzine and I'd see people coming up who I'd seen around Oldham who I never knew were interested in football.'

Nouveau supporters are recklessly ostentatious. They buy everything on sale at the club shop and parade their new love with shameless zeal. Inevitably, they know little of football's culture, or its etiquette. Most fail to appreciate that a football club is for life, not just a metaphorical Christmas. At Oldham, they were dubbed 'Good time Charlies', while at Barnsley, they are known as 'Johnny Come-Latelys'. Barnsley had just 2,500 season ticket-holders last season and a further 5,000 regular supporters who could be considered true to the cause. The club has issued almost 17,000 season tickets this season, which means that the seat next to you at Oakwell is likely to be occupied by a Johnny with a double-barrelled surname.

So far, their loyalty has been absolute and their period of support has embraced a disheartening 6-0 home defeat against Chelsea. Unfortunately, the Oldham experience does not bode well. 'I don't know whether Oldham people are just more fickle than most, but I remember people trying to sell their season ticket just a few months into the first season when we won promotion,' said Mason.

Oldham spent three seasons in the top division, the second two in the newly-inaugurated Premier League, but they were relegated in 1994 and last season slipped down again to the Second Division of the Nationwide League. Supporters believe this rapid demotion was precipitated by the club's policy of selling its better players. 'The place has gone down drastically. I suppose you could say that the rats soon left a sinking ship. I reckon we've kept a tiny proportion of those fans from a few years ago, maybe something like 2 per cent,' said Mason.

Tony Bugby, of the *Oldham Evening Chronicle*, has seen their fall from grace from uncomfortably close quarters. 'There used to be about 40 reporters at the ground on match days. There is probably just half a dozen of us now. Once a club goes into freefall, it is hard to see when it will stop,' he said. Barnsley, of course, feels unique in its delight. It does not want to find the ghost of its Premiership future on the other side of the Pennines. They are right to live for the moment, though an occasional glance at a certain Lancashire club might well be salutary. A life in football can easily go wonky, alas.

---

*Saturday 13 September 1997*

### Barnsley 0 Aston Villa 3

A mediocre Aston Villa side beat Barnsley comprehensively with goals from Ugo Ehiogu, Mark Draper and Ian Taylor. Danny Wilson said his team needed to overcome a psychological barrier. 'It seems that when we come up against teams with big-name players we fail to respond in the right way. It is almost as if they look at the team sheet and fear defeat even before we start,' he said.

---

*Tuesday 16 September 1997*

## Chesterfield 1 Barnsley 2
## (Coca Cola Cup, First Round, First Leg)

Two goals in the final three minutes saved Barnsley from an embarrassing defeat at Chesterfield. Barnsley were awarded a penalty by referee, Paul Danson, but few had spotted an infringement. Neil Redfearn converted and Ashley Ward scored a well-taken winner. Chesterfield had taken the lead from a Tony Lormer penalty after Ales Krizan, making his début, committed a foul in the area. During the match Lars Leese was subject to racial abuse, as the home fans taunted him with chants of 'Stand up if you hate Germans' and 'Let's all shoot a Jerry'.

Earlier in the day, Jovo Bosancic had become a father when his wife, Kim, gave birth to Francesca. The effusive Serbian toured Oakwell throughout the following week informing everyone: 'Every day she gets more beauti-fool', amid much arm-waving. In August, Arjan de Zeeuw had also become a father, naming his daughter Daniek, which his team-mates claimed was a personal tribute to Danny Wilson. Before the end of the season, the partners of Steve Davis, Lars Leese, Ashley Ward and Darren Sheridan all gave birth. 'It shows we are top of the league at something,' joked John Hendrie, himself a father of four.

---

*Wednesday 17 September 1997*

Paul Wilkinson, who had not held down a first-team place, was sold to Millwall for £150,000. 'Paul goes with my best wishes,' said Wilson. 'He is a fantastic professional who has done a fantastic job for us. He is still capable of doing a great job at another level.'

Wilkinson, famed at Oakwell for his red boots, was upset to leave, but, at the age of 33, said he had no alternative. 'At my age I need to be playing in the first team and Millwall offered me that chance. I would have loved to have finished my career at Oakwell,' he said.

———————

*Friday 19 September 1997*

Barnsley's popularity had clearly affected  amateur football in the town. The Barnsley and District Saturday Leagues had shrunk from 40 teams in four divisions to 23 teams in two divisions.

———————

NEW WORLD ON OLD FOUNDATIONS
*(The Times, Saturday 20 September 1997)*

The blinds are half-drawn, so we can see the day see-saw between summer and autumn. A battered car pulls up and a youth steps out. He is wearing a faded T-shirt and long, straggly hair. A middle-aged woman walks her dog across the car park and fastens another button on her anorak as the wind picks up again. Life passes by, quietly, indifferent to the football ground it skirts.

Chris Patzelt – neat, light-coloured suit and Barnsley club tie – stares out across the car park. He smiles, breathes in the tranquillity and remembers the day when bedlam came to Barnsley. It was Saturday 17 May. Pocket diaries will reveal that it was a public holiday in Norway. Patzelt, Barnsley FC's assistant secretary, will tell you that it was a public anguish in Barnsley. Season tickets were available to a select few from 4 May, but on 17 May they went on sale to supporters able to produce ticket stubs from ten of last season's home matches. This would, on the surface, appear to embrace a fairly elite group, but more than 3,000 were queuing outside the ground when Patzelt arrived at 7.30 am. 'I turned around the corner in my car and thought, "Good God", there was nothing else to think really,' he said.

During the previous evening, supporters had arrived at Oakwell with deckchairs, barbecues, crates of beer and sleeping bags. They were offered special passes for the next day to confirm their position at the front of the queue. They declined the offer; mistrust was in the air. 'They actually wanted to stay at the ground overnight. I think they saw it as all part of the romance of promotion,' said Patzelt.

Inevitably, as the deep queue snaked 400 yards around the ground, whispers circulated that tickets were about to run out. Furtive glances were exchanged between fans who feared the good ship Barnsley was to set sail without them.

Some waited for up to 14 hours, but, eventually they all received a ticket. Nearly 17,000 were sold in total, providing more revenue for the club over a few weeks than in the whole of last season.

Patzelt is 37 and has spent all his working life in football. He is one of football's unseen, an administrator. He feels the glow of sporting glamour, but it is from a distance. His world is one of fax machines, letters, invoices, safety drills, police inquiries, press inquiries, inquiries about inquiries. He speaks in the jargon of the trade, of learning curves, contingency plans and prospective revenue figures, but he is also what is termed a 'football man'. He enjoys the gossip of the game. He knows of former professionals who are now driving instructors and Country and Western singers. He can also relate the sequence of scoring in Barnsley's first round, first-leg Coca-Cola Cup tie from a year before, no problem.

Barnsley have risen from relative obscurity to the Premiership because Danny Wilson's successful team has been allied to a solid administrative back-up. 'It is down to good management, good skill, a little bit of luck and a fair degree of stability. A lot of it has really been common sense,' said Patzelt. The club began planning for life in the Premiership at the turn of the year, when the team maintained their position near the top of the First Division. It has created a thousand extra problems, but there has been a rallying call within the club. 'We all answer the phones and we stay until the job is finished.

There's no real demarcation here,' he said.

Barnsley are loyal to the stereotype of much-fabled Yorkshire thriftiness. The impressive East Stand was built for £2.65 million, which is, by today's standards, a good piece of business. 'Other clubs were ringing asking how we got it for that price,' he said, the pride in his voice palpable. 'We only do a deal when it is right. We left it on the table for some time and eventually we got what we considered a good deal.'

The administrative team reports to a board of directors, none of whom draw money from the club. These are traditional, noble patrons of the game, doyens of local family-run firms, each overseeing a separate branch of the club's functions. They are epitomised by John Dennis, club chairman and owner of a fruit and vegetable business. Barnsley have scant trepidation of their new status. Patzelt can talk a good talk; it is his job after all, but there is a seductive charm in his confidence and it permeates the whole club. As he speaks, a lorry passes by carrying asphalt. The car park is being expanded. Another change, and for the better.

---

*Saturday 20 September 1997*

**Everton 4 Barnsley 2**

Danny Cadamarteri, a former schoolboy footballer affiliated to Barnsley, was on the scoresheet for Everton as they recorded a win that was not as comfortable as it appeared. Their other goals were by Gary Speed (two, one a penalty) and John Oster. Neil Redfearn and Darren Barnard replied for Barnsley. David Watson returned in goal. Wilson claimed afterwards that Nick Barmby had 'conned' the referee by diving in the penalty area and winning Everton a spot-kick.

---

*Tuesday 23 September 1997*

## Wimbledon 4 Barnsley 1

The lowest Premiership crowd of the season, just 7,668, saw Barnsley defend gallantly for 65 minutes before conceding four goals in the final 25 minutes. Michael Hughes, Carl Cort, Robbie Earle and Efan Ekoku scored for Wimbledon, after Eric Tinkler had given Barnsley the lead. The defeat was put down to a 'a lack of professionalism and failure to take responsibility' by Wilson. 'It is happening too many times and I am sick of it. It has to stop,' he warned.

The goal proved to be Tinkler's last in a season where he struggled to find fitness and form. *Better Red Than Dead* was particularly uncharitable in its critique of Tinkler: 'His performances on the field have been absolutely abysmal; he can't tackle, can't pass, gets brushed off the ball like he isn't there and for a bloke built like a brick shithouse is about as hard as a marshmallow toasted over an open fire. Yet he struts his stuff as if he's the best player we've ever seen ... I'd rather play Lars Leese in midfield than this streak of cow's piss.'

---

## WHEN LOSING IS NO JOKE
*(The Times, Saturday 27 September 1997)*

Seven weeks ago, Barnsley was a town on helium. The football club had secured promotion to the Premiership and people had sung their joy and eternal loyalty, whether to a television camera, down at the pub, or to the person behind them in the queue for a season ticket.

Since then, the team has lost six matches, conceded 21 goals and finds itself in the relegation zone for the first time this season. There are, of course, thousands who remain unflinchingly loyal, but the trickle of discontent has started. 'It was pretty dire,' wrote John Murphy of Burton Grange, Barnsley. 'We couldn't pass; we didn't know what to do when we had the ball.' It gets worse. 'Barnsley were a pathetic embarrassment, I felt myself cringing in my seat. What is going on at Oakwell?' asked Ellie Hambleton, of Darfield.

These comments were among a batch of letters sent to the *Barnsley Chronicle* after the team's 3-0 home defeat against Aston Villa two weeks ago. At this match, a significant number left ten minutes before the final whistle. Some of these would have been the same people who, back in May, queued for hours to buy a season ticket to ensure that they did not miss out on Barnsley's historic season. Presumably, this air of dissatisfaction will have been honed by two further heavy defeats since.

Much was made of the response to Barnsley's 6-0 drubbing by Chelsea a month ago. They sang when they were hurting, boasting that they were going to win 6-5 when they were five goals behind. The reaction was mere bravado, but it was seen, erroneously, as a barometer of loyalty. When your team is losing so heavily, especially at home, a game takes on a surreal quality. It becomes comical in the same way it does when your luggage flies to Delhi while you land in Rome and the rep announces that there is a meningitis scare at your intended hotel.

It is not a matter of hilarity, however, when your team loses to a struggling Villa side, especially if they have scored three times from eight shots and your team has not scored from 13 attempts. These cruel and frustrating defeats have to be borne reluctantly by the supporter, but with valour. Anything else is cowardly.

Keith Lodge, the sports editor who has opened the letters of complaint at the *Chronicle*, is a seasoned hack, not prone to indignation or shouting. He thinks before he speaks. His response to the grumbling and the early-leavers amounts, then, to a noteworthy reprimand. 'For supporters to dish out such harsh criticism on the management so soon is every bit as pathetic as the embarrassment felt by the lady who sent us a letter describing how she cringed in her seat,' he said.

Malcolm Moyes, a supporter who writes a regular column on Barnsley in a local newspaper, was moved to write: 'It seems to me that a supporter should strengthen the team by sharing the pain and failure, standing by the eleven heroes on the field, not standing up and turning away when things get rough.'

The griping might be premature but it is indicative of a tangible mood-swing within the town. This is mirrored by a degree of change within the club. The side that clinched promotion appears to be disintegrating. In recent games more than half the players used have been signed since the summer. Paul Wilkinson, the striker who formed a 27-goal partnership last season with John Hendrie, has left to join Millwall. Clint Marcelle has been linked with the Spanish club, Seville, and several predatory scouts have noted Hendrie's inability to hold down a first-team place.

Another difference has been Danny Wilson's willingness to publicly criticise his team, notably his defenders. He had previously kept his censure within the dressing-room. This week he called on them in several interviews to 'take on responsibility' and improve their all-round play.

A team in flux, impatient supporters, a manager lambasting his players: Barnsley would seem to be a club bleeding hope and dreams. Everyone knows, though, that a couple of wins, preferably in succession, will have them dancing in the streets once more, such is the fickle nature of the football supporter.

---

*Saturday 27 September 1997*

**Barnsley 0 Leicester City 2**

Danny Wilson switched goalkeepers again and brought in Lars Leese, to no avail. Ian Marshall and Graham Fenton scored in a game where Barnsley showed little fight or imagination.

---

*Tuesday 30 September 1997*

## Barnsley 4 Chesterfield 1
## (Coca Cola Cup, First Round, Second Leg)

Excellent goals by Andy Liddell, Neil Redfearn, Darren Sheridan and Georgi Hristov gave Barnsley a vital boost. Tony Lormor replied once more from the penalty spot for Chesterfield. The attendance was just 8,417 at Oakwell, effectively revealing the team's 'hardcore' support.

# CHAPTER THREE

## The Killing Field

LIFE AT THE TOP

## Rise Of Tea Boy Who Made Good
*(The Times, Saturday 4 October 1997)*

The lines around his brown eyes wrinkle when he smiles. It is a schoolboy's smile, it implores you to share the joke. The eyes do not sparkle, though, when he frowns. They become liquid and stern like a headmaster's. 'I don't suffer fools lightly,' he says, and you believe him.

Danny Wilson is stocky but still possesses the lightness of being shared by all professional sportsmen. He is wearing shorts and has 'DW' stitched into his training top. As he speaks, he lifts his feet on to a small table in the boardroom. 'They've been great to me, this lot,' he said, pointing to the photographs of the club's directors mounted on the wall. 'They are all really into their football.'

He talks freely, trusting a reporter's notebook in the same way he would someone sitting next to him on a train. Such absence of edifice and caution is charming. The world closes in to a single room, a pot of tea and his distinct pleasure in conversation. There is none of the habitual 'hurry-hurry, here's your quotes, there's the door'.

Barnsley have made a poor start to their first season in the Premiership and are already enmeshed in a relegation battle that most observers felt was inevitable. Wilson remains chipper all the same, and he has greater concerns than football to shadow his days. His mother, Annie, who attended almost every game in which he was involved, either as player or manager, died shortly after the season began. 'She was a lovely woman, so friendly and so patient. You've got to keep those things to yourself though. I suppose that's a Northern trait, you harden up,' he said.

Wilson began his working life as a tea boy at Ravenhead brickworks, close to his home town of Billinge, near Wigan. His father, Jim 'Tug' Wilson, also worked there as a forklift truck driver. Wilson had signed associate schoolboy forms with Sunderland, but had not been offered an apprenticeship. His return to professional football was reminiscent of a story drawn from a schoolboy football annual. A shadowy figure in an overcoat arrived one afternoon at the brickworks. The stranger was Bobby Smith, then manager of Bury. He persuaded Wilson Sr that his son should leave the brickworks and become a footballer. 'My dad was old school. I think he told Bobby he didn't mind at all, as long as he made sure I was disciplined and did as I was told,' said Wilson.

He made his début at 17 and it was the start of a playing career spanning 18 years, eight clubs, all four divisions, and 24 international caps for Northern Ireland. He has been described as a journeyman footballer and if this is the epithet for consistency, allied to a certain neatness of play, then it is apt. Football insiders believe his playing days were fundamentally an apprenticeship for a starring role as a manager. He was hungry to learn and his mentors ranged from the famous to the unsung. He played under Brian Clough at Nottingham Forest and Ron Atkinson at Sheffield Wednesday, but he mentions other names that are less familiar; men who, quietly but indelibly, shape the character of a football club.

Since he has spent much of his career in Yorkshire and has appeared for Northern Ireland, there is ambiguity about Wilson's roots. He will have none of it and feels he is stamped 'Made in Lancashire.' His parents met while his father was serving with the Royal Navy in Northern Ireland. Annie lived in Londonderry, where Jim played as a full-back for Derry City. The couple married and moved to the small, semi-rural town of Billinge, between Wigan and St Helens, an area of flat land that runs to the Irish Sea. Wilson is remembered fondly in the town.

'There's a lot of Wigan in him. We don't crow about things from the rooftops. We just get on with the job,' said Mick Hannan. He knew Wilson in the 1970s when they were both involved in amateur football. Wilson played for Double Seven youth club, a team affiliated to Wigan Athletic.

Wilson exudes an aura of calm and integrity. In conversation, he refers continually to trust, honesty and commitment. During his short time in management, he has surrounded himself with people loyal to this mantra. 'I like to suss out someone's character, to listen to what they have to say. I very rarely rant and rave. I believe in the adage that if you want to be heard, you should speak quietly,' he said.

Viv Anderson, now assistant manager at Middlesbrough, brought Wilson to Barnsley as his own assistant when he became manager in 1993. He recommended that Wilson should replace him when he left a year later. 'Danny is intelligent and works hard. He is a very straight-talking person – what you see is what you get. He is very principled,' said Anderson.

Barnsley take on Arsenal, the Premiership leaders, at Highbury today. It is another challenge in a challenging season. Wilson has been here before, it is merely the scenery that has changed. Back in 1974, Wigan Athletic B were losing 3-0 at half-time against Hindley Town in the Subsidiary Cup final. Wilson was just 14 and came on as a substitute. The score? 4-3 for Wigan Athletic B, all the goals made by Wilson.

---

*Saturday 4 October 1997*

### Arsenal 5 Barnsley 0

Barnsley held out for the first 25 minutes but then had no response to a slick Arsenal whose goals were scored by Dennis Bergkamp (two), Ray Parlour, David Platt and Ian Wright. Many other teams were outclassed by Arsenal during the course of their season, but it was the fifth time in 10 Premiership matches that Barnsley had conceded three or more goals. They fell to the bottom of the league for the first time.

Danny Wilson used a term he was to call upon a few times over the next few weeks. 'It has to be said, our defending is pathetic at times – a joke. And it has to be sorted out,' he grumbled.

---

*Monday 6 October 1997*

A local fitness expert, Peter Willey, wrote to the club offering to pass on a training routine devised by his father. Michael Spinks, the club's secretary/general manager, assumed the offer was spoof and responded: 'Dear Mr Sweatbox ...' Mr Willey was not amused.

————————

### ACCENT THAT RESONATES AT OAKWELL
*(The Times, Saturday 11 October 1997)*

Bottles of mineral water stand on the top table and there is a pen and a notebook in front of each of the five seats. A huge Radio 5 Live banner is draped across the concrete breeze-blocks painted job-lot magnolia.

David Mellor strides into the room, past microphone stands and supporters in their team colours. Players in the red of Barnsley stare down from team photographs on the wall. The squad of 1978-79 look like an anthropological exhibit of an ancient race of footballers; all loose-ring perms, wiry moustaches and skinny, boyish bodies. The last time Mellor was in Barnsley, he was prowling the town centre, looking for old ladies willing to offer a hand to shake, or young mothers with babies to fuss over. Where he once solicited votes for the Conservative Party, he now seeks the voice of the authentic football supporter. 'Come on, have your say,' he implores, and the airwaves are yours, if there is sufficient time between his next discourse and the 8 o'clock news.

While the executive suite at Oakwell hosts this latest 'football forum', there is a hullabaloo taking place in another Northern town, a 90-minute drive to the west. Ffion Jenkins, fiancée of William Hague, the Leader of the Opposition, has taken the conservative out of Conservatism with the help of an immodest black dress at the party's annual conference. So, Blackpool is on fire, awash with flashlights, drunk on the romance of renaissance. Meanwhile, the nation's ultimate renaissance man is missing the festivities because he is in Barnsley, in cuff-links.

A football forum is an itinerant talking-shop where Mellor gets to play shopkeeper. A smart shopkeeper he is too, in an outfit he might well proffer as a potential Chelsea strip: blue shirt with pin stripes, white collar and cuffs, and, of course, glittering cuff-links. Alongside him is a quietly charismatic panel rich in football acumen: Danny Wilson; Chris Kamara, the Bradford City manager; Steve Nicol, the Sheffield Wednesday defender, and Mark Lawrenson, the former professional turned pundit. The audience has been selected judiciously. They are polite, informed, attentive, the kind of people who know that the plural of stadium is stadia.

They have submitted their questions beforehand and these have been typed out by someone at the radio station, so they can be read aloud when a microphone is swung over their head. The clapping at the start is ominously reminiscent of *Gardeners' Question Time*. Wilson, as host, is the focus of the early queries. He is not born to the spotlight, and it finds him reluctantly. He says 'in all honesty' and 'at this moment in time' rather a lot, but between the clichés there are words of sincerity and assurance. In answer to the question, at this moment in time he does not know, in all honesty, whether Barnsley are equipped to survive in the Premiership.

Lawrenson plays the comic and his irreverence is a necessary foil to Mellor's pontificating. The panel members are remarkably acquiescent to the chairman, their demeanour suggesting that they feel like schoolboys in the presence of the headmaster. He knows more words than they do, has a posh accent, and where they are apprehensive of the microphone, he adores it.

The issues discussed are typical fare: referees, a proposed mid-winter break, stewarding, a return to terraces, and racism in the game. Mellor, by mistake, brings someone into the discussion out of turn. A lady with a clipboard waves her arms and shakes her head. He follows her command, but, behind her back, glowers with enough vehemence to make Dennis Bergkamp mis-hit in front of an open goal.

Mellor, to give him his due, is not without a sense of humour, though the best one-liner of the evening belongs to Lawrenson, with a creditable assist from Wilson. Ian O'Brien, of Wakefield, asks whether footballers are fair to their fans, citing a recent visit to the Liverpool training ground where he saw a player drive through a group of children waiting for his autograph. 'At Barnsley we chase after the kids and make them have our autographs,' says Wilson. 'That's if you can catch them,' adds Lawrenson.

John Dennis, the Barnsley chairman, is spotted in the corridor afterwards, looking distinctly proud that Barnsley has been visited by a national radio station. Perhaps next time, though, the forum should be held in Barnsley market or at one of the town's working men's clubs. And no-one gets to see the questions first.

---

### Saturday 11 October 1997

Georgi Hristov (Macedonia), Ales Krizan (Slovenia) and Eric Tinkler (South Africa) were all on international duty as their countries played matches against Lithuania, Croatia and France respectively.

---

### Tuesday 14 October 1997

**Barnsley 1 Southampton 2
(Coca Cola Cup Third Round)**

Barnsley played well but a superb goal by Matt Le Tissier and a winner against the run-of-play by Kevin Davies secured Southampton's victory. Andy Liddell scored for Barnsley. The attendance of 9,019 was again significantly below the Premiership level, though this was commonplace for a cup competition that increasingly failed to capture the supporters' imagination.

## WHERE WATCHING A GAME IS AGONY
*(The Times, Saturday 18 October 1997)*

The request seems reasonable enough. 'Bugger off,' snaps John Dennis, the chairman of Barnsley and a wholesale greengrocer. He does not want to share his working day with anyone, especially a journalist, thank you very much. He offers a compromise: 'You can have an hour. I'll see you at 3 o'clock at the club.' Would he like a phone call on the day to remind him? He is affronted: 'No, I'll be there.'

At 2.55 pm he drives his smart Audi into the club car park and walks nonchalantly towards the reception area, a burly figure in a black overcoat. His skin is doughy, he seldom smiles; there is something of the undertaker about his demeanour. Some Barnsley supporters are queueing for tickets at the box office. He passes by unnoticed. He is already more than ten hours into a working day that starts at 4.30 am, the time when produce arrives at his company headquarters in Pontefract Road, Barnsley. It is then distributed by staff of about a hundred to shops and markets in a 60-mile radius. 'I don't know how he does it,' said Danny Wilson, commenting on his chairman's stamina.

'I'm overweight, stressed, I smoke too much and I like the odd tipple,' said Dennis. He also swears a good deal more than your average club chairman. He is public school educated, but has spent all his life in Barnsley, a town that does not stand on ceremony. 'John is very down to earth. He cares passionately about the club and has a real affinity with the town,' said an insider. 'He will stand his corner, but sometimes takes a bad result too much to heart. He has a really bad weekend if we lose.'

Within the game, Dennis is known for his self-assurance and a certain brusque charm. He accepts praise with the same scepticism he holds for reproach. He is a Yorkshireman, which is, by common definition, a warm heart beating in an icy exterior. Wilson has often spoke of his fondness. 'That's because I'm a soft touch!' jokes Dennis.

Dennis has had to temper his natural ebullience. A few years ago he found himself in a fury outside the dressing-room of a referee who had sent off a Barnsley player. 'I was seething and went down to give the ref a volley,' he said. 'When he opened the door to me I thought, you prat, what are you going to do now? It was a pointless way to achieve anything and I realised then that I would have to go about things in a different way.'

The qualities that have taken Barnsley to the Premiership are distilled in Dennis. He is a pragmatist, hard-working and loyal, quietly charismatic, organised and unwilling to accept a natural order that would see Barnsley down among the dead men of English football. He will take his place in the VIP seats at Old Trafford next Saturday when Barnsley visit the champions, excited but undaunted. 'We're in this division because our results say we are good enough to be here,' he said. So there.

He inherited his love of the club from his father, Ernest, the club chairman from 1967 until his death in July 1979. The first game John attended at Oakwell was a 0-0 draw against Derby County in the 1958-59 season, an inauspicious start since Barnsley were relegated at the end of the season to the old Third Division. 'I've given up trying to explain why I support Barnsley. It is just something that gets under your skin,' he said.

These days, he has invested so much time and emotion into Barnsley that the simple pleasure of watching them play is denied. 'Watching the games is agony. Ninety minutes are very stressful. I only relax when we've won,' he said. A comfortable lead does not alleviate the tension and he recalls – in gruesomely assiduous detail – two games where three-goal leads were squandered. 'I suppose if we were 8-0 up with 15 minutes left I might relax a bit,' he said.

His most important decision was to appoint Wilson as manager in the summer of 1994. Wilson had been assistant to Viv Anderson, who left to join Middlesbrough. The supporters wanted new blood and were unhappy with Wilson's promotion. 'He was always the obvious choice for me. He has an excellent reputation and is determined. He is full of character and has a deep knowledge of the game,' said Dennis. The appointment paid off handsomely when, on Saturday 26 April of this year, Barnsley secured promotion to the top flight with a 2-0 win against Bradford City. Amid the euphoria, there was a private, tender moment for Dennis. Johnny Steele, an ex-Barnsley player and a manager (on two separate occasions) for a total of 12 seasons, passed him in the stand. The two Barnsley stalwarts had the same thought. 'I know who you are thinking about,' said Steele. John Dennis was thinking of his father and a dream realised.

———————

While I was interviewing Dennis, our photographer arrived at reception to take his picture. The chairman was obviously enjoying our conversation, and declined to break off for the photograph. My plan was to strike a rapport with Dennis and, because the interview was going well, I did not want to interrupt him. This was obviously unfair on the photographer, but newspaper people respect that in these situations there is an element of 'every man for himself'. It was up to Dennis how he responded to the constant reminders that someone was waiting for him.

The photographer was left in a small, dull room for nearly two hours without even a chair to sit on, or the offer of a cup of tea. He thought that our interview might end at any minute, so did not return to his car in case Dennis left Oakwell on his blindside. When Dennis did appear, he was only prepared to spend a few minutes having his picture taken. The photographer said afterwards that it was the worst he had been treated by a football club, and he had covered bigger clubs than Barnsley.

At the time, there had been many demands on Dennis from the media, and it is possible that he had briefly become a touch blasé of the attention. On other occasions, though, he was, without exception, prepared to interrupt his working day to field my questions in his usual direct, candid manner. 'Is this off the record?' he would ask. He would then speak with the veracity of a fan: 'Yeah, I agree, he's crap.' Or, when asked for his view on a certain football pundit: 'Don't ask me about that obnoxious ...'

The dismissive treatment of the photographer might have been an aberration, though the club's haphazard approach to public relations would suggest otherwise. The job of PR appeared to fall upon several members of staff, though none were trained specifically or were particularly adept. They had to fit in dealing with the media around their other tasks. In confidence, I was told by other journalists that their reluctance to employ designated PR staff was two-fold. Firstly, the club was reluctant to allocate finance and, secondly, 'It's like a bloody secret society, always has been!'

Sometimes, the lackadaisical approach worked in my favour. I was able to gain access easily and unimpinged. At other clubs, I might have found myself conducting an interview with a star striker where an agent or PR officer tut-tutted or piped up every five minutes: 'Out of bounds.' At Barnsley, life is more straightforward: you cadge a player's home number, phone them, and arrange to meet at a hotel or service station. They talk to you openly; some, for example, will even tell you how much they earn.

On other occasions, the lack of personnel with knowledge of the media's requirements was frustrating. There seemed to be no-one willing to make a decision, except when the request was complex or required a little thought; then the response was invariably in the negative, it made for an easier life. During the season, the club survived on a great deal of goodwill, so professional PR staff did not seem a priority.

Obviously, it is vital that the club maintains its character and does not suddenly reinvent itself as Barnsley Have-A-Nice-Day-Sir FC, but, likewise, the media – and hence, the public – expect a better service. Most Premiership clubs have a PR department, some staffed by up to four people. If Barnsley aspires to the same level of professionalism, it needs to embrace the PR age, on its own terms.

———

*Monday 20 October 1997*

**Barnsley 2 Coventry City 0**

A disheartening run of six consecutive league defeats ended with a victory against Coventry City. Ashley Ward and Neil Redfearn (penalty) secured the win after David Watson had made a string of saves. It was Barnsley's biggest win of the season and the only time that they beat a team by more than a one-goal margin. It lifted them two places from the foot of the table. The squad had been putting in extra training sessions, working on team pattern and organisation in the morning and fitness in the afternoon.

---

*Friday 24 October 1997*

On the eve of Barnsley's visit to Old Trafford to take on league-leaders Manchester United, Danny Wilson issued the obligatory fighting talk. 'We are not just going to roll over for our belly to be tickled. We're going to give them a game,' he said.

---

SHERIDAN CENTRE STAGE AT THE THEATRE OF DREAMS
*(The Times, Saturday 25 October 1997)*

Old Trafford is busy as usual. We are still a few days away from the next match but people mill around holding carrier bags bulging with Manchester United paraphernalia. Darren Sheridan, shoulders rolling, walks through the throng unnoticed. He is a short, stocky man with an unpretentious manner and an unpretentious haircut, one of those that is the preserve of barbers of a certain age who smoke while they work, cough into the back of your neck, and have more opinions than they do clean combs.

'I'm playing at Old Trafford on Saturday,' Sheridan tells his coughing coiffeur. 'Aye, and I'm singing with Frank Sinatra the weekend after next,' is the retort. 'It's a dream come true, isn't it?' says Sheridan, for the third time in ten minutes. Footballers make statements like that all the time. Everything is a dream come true – the last goal, the next game, the impending transfer, the sponsorship deal with Reebok. The difference is that this is the real thing. A Mancunian and a Manchester United supporter, he will take his place in the Barnsley team against United at Old Trafford today. If he looks more like a postman, baker, warehouseman or labourer than he does a footballer, it is no coincidence because, at various times, he was all of those until a few years ago.

Like his elder brother, John, Sheridan was an apprentice footballer with Leeds United. While John went on to play regularly for Leeds and later with Sheffield Wednesday and Bolton Wanderers, Darren was released at 18 by Billy Bremner, the then Leeds manager. 'I thought that was the end of it,' said Sheridan. 'I believed it when I was told I wasn't good enough. John was always saying I could make it in football, but I suppose I just gave up.'

After a stint playing for a pub team in Stretford, Sheridan was picked up by Winsford United, of the UniBond League, where he spent four seasons. During this period he held various jobs on short contracts and watched Manchester United as often as possible. On one occasion he was out of work and offered to call at the shops for bread and milk for his mother. On his way he met two friends about to board a train to London for a United game against Arsenal. 'I got £60 out of the bank and went with them. I ended up swinging this bloody loaf around my head on the terraces. My mam wasn't happy when I got back!' he said.

Seven years after his rejection by Leeds, Sheridan finally became a professional footballer when he was offered a contract by Barnsley in 1993. He had to leave the Dannimac warehouse in Trafford Park, Manchester, where he worked in stock control.

He has been a fixture in Barnsley's midfield for the past three seasons, where his combative, scurrying approach has formed a protective vanguard for Barnsley's more expansive play. The opponent in his path today is likely to be David Beckham, and the contrast could not be greater. While Beckham dates a Spice Girl, Sheridan lives modestly within a mile of Old Trafford with his girlfriend, Jannette, and their two young daughters. Beckham has the patronage of pan-global companies while Sheridan is happy that a floor-covering firm sponsors his kit. Beckham's annual income will be at least 15 times greater than Sheridan's, but they will be equals for the 90 minutes on the pitch today.

Sheridan describes himself as a 'biter around the ankles' player and he will be doing just that against United. 'I don't feel out of place at all, me. I love it. I think we've got to get nastier as a team, if you know what I mean. There are some very clever players in the league and we've got to get among them. I think we've been showing them too much respect,' he said.

Off the pitch, Sheridan is notoriously laid-back, to the point of not knowing the surname of some of his team-mates. 'I couldn't say half of the names of the foreign lads even if I could remember,' he said. 'I just say: "Hey, give me the ball," and they usually do.' He also has problems with the Yorkshire dialect spoken in Barnsley. 'It cracks me up,' he said. 'They come up to me and tell me I'm a chuffin' good player or a reet good 'un.' He smiles constantly, as if, between speaking, he is telling himself private jokes. It is not an expression of conceit; in fact, it is quite endearing. 'Wouldn't you be smiling?' he asks. 'One minute I'm in a warehouse working all hours, and now I'm about to play at Old Trafford. It's a dream come true, isn't it?' There he goes again.

---

*Saturday 25 October 1997*

**Manchester United 7 Barnsley 0**

Manchester United played some mesmeric football against Barnsley, and seemed able to score at will. They eventually won 7-0, though it could have been more. Neil Thompson, the

Barnsley defender, had been a member of the Ipswich Town which had lost 9-0 at Old Trafford a few years earlier. United's goals were scored by Andy Cole (three), Ryan Giggs (two), Paul Scholes and Karel Poborsky. 'Our defending was laughable. We committed suicide,' said Wilson.

---

HOPES PERISH ON BARNSLEY'S PEAK
*(match report, The Times, Monday 27 October 1997*

A light smattering of frost covered much of northern England on Saturday and there was a distinct chill in the air. The calendar merely confirmed the obvious; the official end of British Summer Time.

After this comprehensive and cruel defeat, it would also appear to be the end of Barnsley's summer time. They ran into Manchester United in scintillating form and, despite their best intentions, were left bewildered, like accident victims meandering around a hospital casualty department.

'I didn't get a sniff of any of the goals,' said David Watson, the Barnsley goalkeeper. All he and his team-mates were left with was the unpleasant odour of a heavy defeat and professional humiliation. They were extras in a United performance that finally warranted Old Trafford's sniffy sobriquet, the Theatre of Dreams. The Barnsley players had just two roles – to run around valiantly, but pointlessly, and then hang their heads low when the ball went into their net.

'There is a great confidence coming into the club,' said Alex Ferguson, the United manager. 'We are just on song, absolutely on song. You get performances like this once or twice a season. I don't think you could fault a single Barnsley player. They just didn't have an answer to the speed of our attacks.'

Barnsley were allowed custody of the ball for long periods, but they were largely reduced to shuffling sideways across midfield. United, in contrast, tore forward, the ball moving from player to player almost too quickly for the naked eye. Before the game, Barnsley had promised to remain undaunted and unafraid of their illustrious opponents. This was not even an issue; United were a lizard's tail, impossible to grasp, always two moves ahead, the ball skittering towards the Barnsley penalty area. Neil Redfearn, the Barnsley captain, cajoled his team-mates and chased every shadow that flickered across his path, but the toil he epitomised was worthless and became effort merely for its own sake against such sublime artistry. When Barnsley did fleetingly encroach on United's private party and trade tackles, they were invariably stung by the speed of thought, the touch of genius, that left them apoplectic, their hands on hips, their hearts in their boots.

United have aspired to greatness for many years and, for 90 minutes on Saturday, it was irrefutably attained. Critics will say that it was only Barnsley, but Barnsley are of the same division and they were made to look like lost souls in football shirts. The game was decidedly stodgy until the first goal after 17 minutes. Sheridan stroked the ball between two of his defenders and, while they held a meeting to discuss who should collect it, Cole raced in and placed it defiantly past Watson. Barnsley's team spirit has been much exulted this season, but the hostile manner in which first de Zeeuw and then Eaden berated Sheridan would suggest that perfidy has found a foothold.

Within 90 seconds, Cole had scored again and Giggs made it three just a few minutes before half-time. Loyal to the theory of negating Giggs, Barnsley shepherded him across the pitch on to his right foot, but he still had the mastery to pound the ball into the net from distance. Cole completed his hat-trick seconds before the interval with another piece of exemplary finishing.

During the break, the Barnsley supporters were informed that their coaches had been moved from Elevator Road to Waters Edge, an area by the Manchester Ship Canal. The inherent sadism of locating a group of disheartened Barnsley fans in close proximity to a large expanse of water obviously escaped the announcer. Barnsley held out for 12 minutes after half-time before Giggs scored again, followed by Scholes and, finally, Poborsky, who set his feet dancing to elude the defence and place the ball contemptuously beyond the goalkeeper.

Danny Wilson was chipper despite the scoreline and this will be a capital asset during his team's winter of discontent. It means we will be spared the habitual moping and moaning that accompanies such a tortuous ordeal. 'There was nothing between the teams apart from seven goals,' he joked. 'United's team is full of high-class players and they take some stopping when they work up a head of steam. They seemed to be able to score at will.'

Many Barnsley fans travelled straight to Blackpool after the match, intent on a pleasurable weekend, regardless of the result. This kind of defiance will keep alive the optimism of a long hot summer during a long, cold winter.

---

*Monday 27 October 1997*

Dean Jones, a 20-year-old defender who had appeared several times for the reserves, tested positive for amphetamine at the club's training ground. He was charged with misconduct by the FA and given 14 days to respond. He was suspended immediately by Barnsley. 'We deplore the use of drugs and are fully supportive of the FA's stance,' said John Dennis. Although Jones had not appeared for the first team, or indeed travelled with the squad, he was registered as a Barnsley player and so became the first footballer with a Premiership club to face such a charge.

Another reserve defender, Mark Hume, aged 19, appeared in Barnsley Magistrates' Court after admitting a speeding offence. He was caught travelling at 63 mph in a 30 mph zone. He was fined £88 with £40 court costs.

---

*Tuesday 27 October 1997*

Barnsley announced operating profits of £383,627 during their promotion season. It was also revealed that the wage bill had increased from £1,541,947 to £2,398,957, while £4,617,940 had been spent on transfer fees since promotion. Clearly, the club had embarked upon a programme of qualified speculation.

———————

## OPTIMISM DIES WITH BARNSLEY
*(The Times, Saturday 1 November 1997)*

When the kicking and screaming is over, and the good people are back in their homes, a football ground is left to its own peculiar solitude. Silence is infinitely louder in places that have recently been alive with noise and energy, places such as Old Trafford on a Saturday evening.

Just a few hours earlier, it had been a metropolis of restless hubbub but, by nightfall, it was half-asleep in the half-light. Silvery clouds were picked out against the sky by a glow of orange, while darkness consorted with a mist encroaching from the Manchester Ship Canal. On this cold, damp evening, the world seemed to stand still, and walking away from Manchester United felt like walking away from a wake.

It is only football, of course, but football is sport and sport is a celebration of life. Barnsley did not so much lose against United, they died, and slipping into the eternal night with them was every dreamer and optimist who had invested so much in this impudent football club from provincial England. When Barnsley clinched promotion to the Premiership, the response across the country was extraordinary. We are a nation that covets the underdog and, in Barnsley, we had found the apogee of this obsession. On that mild day in April when Barnsley defeated Bradford City to ensure promotion, we rejoiced because this was a corner-shop team, homespun and small-town, set to take on the conglomerates of Arsenal, Liverpool and Manchester United. Hope and optimism had suddenly made a comeback.

On Saturday, as United flattened Barnsley to record a 7-0 win, our idealism was mocked, our hopes made foolhardy. The scoreline did not flatter United; it could have been greater.

'The Killing Field' was the headline in the *Manchester Evening News* and it was apropriate to the circumstances. The match was uncomfortable to watch; United played with a glee that bordered on misanthropy and toyed with their opponents. A towel thrown from the Barnsley bench would have been a merciful release.

Such emphatic scorelines were reserved previously for cup matches, when top teams were drawn against the grafting journeymen of non-league or lower-league football. A bunch of craggy-faced, barrel-chested blokes would charge around purposefully but vainly and lose 8-0 to the sleek, moustachioed professionals in tight shorts. There was a natural order, all was well with the world. Barnsley's defeat is all the more onerous because they are of the same division as United. When a team can inflict such cynical damage on a supposed equal, all is far from well. It basically condemns Barnsley and their ilk to a ghetto at the bottom of the league, where the only respite from defeat upon defeat is the occasional win against Coventry City or Bolton Wanderers. Promotion seems futile and merely a gangplank along which only sadists and fools would wish to walk.

The men in tracksuits charged with motivating teams such as Barnsley often jab the ribs of their young bulls and remind them, 'They've only got two legs and two arms, just like you'. This is true, of course, but such livestock has been collected from around the world at any price and nurtured with startling intensity. It would appear that there is not a player, nor indeed a schoolboy footballer, who has not been assessed by the all-seeing eye of Manchester United.

Most of the Barnsley team would be pushed to claim a place in United's reserve team, such is their surfeit of talent. Ronnie Wallwork and John Curtis, two of United's reserves, both played against Barnsley and immediately looked as if they were born to such a prestigious stage. No team is infallible, and, on any given day, the excessively moneyed teams will be beaten by the also-rans. Where this might have once happened on, say, a monthly basis, it will now occur as frequently as a snowstorm in June.

Shelagh Delaney, the playwright born just a few miles from Old Trafford, might have been summarising Barnsley's predicament in a scene drawn from her slice-of-life drama, *A Taste of Honey*. The play's main character, Jo, a gawky, unattractive teenager, meets Jimmy, a sailor, while he is on shore leave. Her life is suddenly flushed by romance and a tinge of the exotic. Jimmy departs, without leaving a forwarding address, and Jo discovers she's pregnant. 'The dream has gone, but the baby is real,' she laments.

———————

The fatalistic tone of that article was perhaps over-done, but on the evening of the defeat it really did feel so hopeless and pointless. In hindsight, the piece did not emphasise that United's exhilarating form would inevitably have a limited lifespan. No team could play such perfect football for anything more than a few matches. It was flawless, dream football. Also, sport, whatever the circumstances, has the facility of recuperation and renewal, as later games against Manchester United confirmed.

CHAPTER FOUR

My Brother Grim

*Saturday 1 November 1997*

## Barnsley 1 Blackburn Rovers 1

Barnsley rallied after a disappointing first-half performance which had caused the Oakwell crowd to barrack the team for the first time in the season. Jovo Bosancic scored for Barnsley and Tim Sherwood for Rovers, who were third in the league at the time. Afterwards, Bosancic revealed that Wilson had delivered another broadside at the interval. 'I think it is better I do not tell you what Danny Wilson said at half-time,' he told reporters.

---

*Wednesday 5 November 1997*

David Pleat was sacked as manager of Sheffield Wednesday and Danny Wilson found himself linked immediately with a return to the club for whom he had played nearly 100 games before his arrival at Oakwell. 'He is here. And he is staying,' said John Dennis.

---

### FORMER STRIKER OFFERS SPIRITUAL GUIDANCE
*(The Times, Saturday 8 November 1997)*

The woolly jumper comes off at an alarming speed and is replaced by a replica Barnsley shirt. The Rev Peter Amos pats out a few creases and looks immediately at ease, born to the role. The strip of grass outside Ward Green baptist church in Barnsley has been turned into a makeshift football pitch by local youths and stones mark out rough goalposts. It is a tempting sight. Now dressed for the occasion, the plea is expected at any minute: 'Come on, let's have a kickabout,' as the reverend produces a football secreted among the bibles and prayer books.

Amos is the club chaplain of Barnsley FC, a position he has

held for four years. The previous incumbent was Charlie McKenzie, a man known affectionately as 'Charlie Chaplain'. That a football club should have an ecclesiastical link is invariably viewed with scepticism, yet nearly half of all English clubs have made such an appointment, including Manchester United. A club is ultimately a community, after all.

'When we first started there was a tremendous amount of suspicion,' said Amos. 'Most of the hangers-on at a football club are there for something they can get out of it but when people are there to give, they cannot understand it.' He visits the club every Thursday and spends about two hours wandering through the offices, stadium and training area. 'I talk to every one, from the lady who washes the kit to spending five minutes with Danny Wilson. I try to help people keep perspective. A person's health, well-being and soul can be distorted by a continual emphasis on one area of their lives, as it is with football,' he said.

As an amateur footballer, Amos was a striker with various clubs for 30 years and is quietly proud of his goals-per-game ratio. His career ended on a hugely embarrassing note when he was booked for the first time in his final match. 'I was booked for talking to the referee. I was always one for a chat with the ref during the game,' he said.

Middlesbrough, his home town club, were his first love and the first game he attended at Oakwell was when Middlesbrough were the visitors. Afterwards he found his loyalties transferred and along with his wife, Jean, and four daughters, he became a regular at Barnsley. Wilson has been exulted in the town but few people have been allowed the insight which Amos has gained. 'I have rarely seen anyone live under the kind of pressure this season has brought to him and handle it so well,' he said. 'Danny would say it is not pressure at all, and that bringing up five kids on £80 a week is real pressure. He has a tremendously relaxed attitude and a great deal of integrity.'

Earlier this week, Wilson was linked with the vacant managerial post at Sheffield Wednesday. Amos doubts whether Wilson would accept the job but, even so, feels there would be little animosity if he were to defect to local rivals: 'I think our fans will understand that Danny came from Sheffield Wednesday in the first place. There are bigger and better clubs than us and we recognise that anyone with ambition is likely to move at some point.'

When Barnsley secured promotion last season, there was a sense of a dream fulfilled, that simply being part of the Premiership was enough in itself. Inevitably, as the team has struggled against the sheer quality of opposition, some grumbling has ensued. 'We achieve our dreams but when we get there it is not as expected,' Amos said. 'It cannot be found in worldly things. It is a spiritual ache at the heart of people that is not being fulfilled.'

He feels his most important function as club chaplain is to place football in its proper context; that it can be joyous and uplifting, but it is part of life, not a life in itself. As he waits to have his photograph taken he instinctively adopts the posture of a footballer, almost running on the spot. He has remained fit through regular jogs and walks in the stunning countryside around Barnsley. His childhood hero was Denis Law and they share the same colouring and sense of fun. In the hallway of the church is a noticeboard on which people have pinned notes asking the congregation to pray for loved ones. Philip has leukaemia and 'hopefully will soon be in remission'; Debbie and Daniel have a 'seriously ill baby'; June has had a stroke at 36; Dave has 'had a brain op'. Sometimes life has its own way of putting football into perspective.

---

*Saturday 8 November 1997*

**Southampton 4 Barnsley 1**

Barnsley conceded a goal in the third minute when Adie Moses was ruled to have fouled Kevin Davies. Matt Le Tissier converted the penalty and Carlton Palmer added a second a few minutes later. Davies scored the third before half-time but Jovo

Bosancic replied for Barnsley from the penalty spot; Neil Redfearn, the usual penalty-taker, missed the game through a heavy cold. David Hirst, a former Barnsley apprentice who had made 26 appearances for the first team back in 1985-86, scored Southampton's fourth goal.

Danny Wilson was furious with the team and several players commented that they had never seen him lose his temper to such a degree before. The defeat meant a return to the bottom of the league after a three-week break. 'I felt anger boiling up inside me throughout the game,' explained Wilson. 'And it finally reached boiling point. Players are accepting defeat too easily, almost as if it doesn't matter to them. Well it matters to me.' On a more portentous note, Wilson added: 'I am beginning to doubt the qualities of the players for the first time since I came here.'

---

*Tuesday 11 November 1997*

Ashley Ward was diagnosed as having viral meningitis and admitted to a hospital in Manchester under observation. When he returned to Oakwell a few days later, he was asked if he had enjoyed the 'rest'. He complained that there had been nine others in the ward with him, including an old lady with severe flatulence. He had not had a wink of sleep during his two-day stay.

---

*Wednesday 12 November 1997*

Nine first-team regulars played for the reserves in a nil-nil draw against Lincoln City at Oakwell. Again, there were few signs of players finding their form and only a late miss by Lincoln saved Barnsley from an ignominious defeat.

---

*Tuesday 18 November 1997*

The Barnsley first team squad visited Anfield to watch Liverpool take on Grimsby Town in a Coca Cola Cup tie. Wilson thought it important to sample the atmosphere at the famous ground, so it would not seem so strange or intimidating when they returned four days later. Liverpool won 3-0, but were not overly impressive.

———————

*Friday 21 November 1997*

On the eve of Barnsley's match with Liverpool, Wilson ordered the players on to the team coach. They drove a mile from their hotel and called at a pub where they were told they could have a couple of pints each. They met up with several locals who teased them that they would need more than two pints to summon the courage to face Liverpool. The players appreciated Wilson's gesture and said it helped them relax before the big match. Afterwards, it was seen as a psychological masterstroke by Wilson.

———————

EFFORTS TO REFINE THE TALK OF THE TOWN
*(The Times, Saturday 22 November 1997)*

The Mullahs of marketing relish a challenge. They sit around swivel-top tables fuelling inspiration with numerous cups of coffee. After much chin-stroking and brow-furrowing their caffeine-kindled schemes catch fire and, hey presto, the dream is yours, at a price.

Before they can sell the idea, they have to sell the name. If your client happens to be called Barnsley, this is where the enigma begins. 'I think it's just the way it is pronounced by the locals. I mean, Barnet is a similar word, but the rounded 'a' means it sounds OK,' said Jim Stringer, senior copywriter at Cicero, one of the leading advertising agencies in the North.

Barnsley, especially in the South Yorkshire tongue, does sound undeniably downbeat. The vowel in the first syllable is flat and long, while the second syllable is clipped. Phonetically, it would be spelt: 'Baarns-li'. To aggravate matters, Barnsley is stuck with an image as a grim, soot-blackened town where the cornerstones of life – birth, school, work, death – are played out in a drab, monotonous tone. Its 225,000 residents know full well how their town is perceived, and, though they may claim not to care, they are affronted and hurt. In fact, much of the town's character – warm but weary, stoical but sentimental – is shaped by this eternal 'us and them' perspective.

Football has finally supplied a fingerhold on the kind of glamour that Barnsley covets. When Barnsley FC were promoted to the Premiership, hope and self-esteem sweetened the daily grind. Barnsley's tourist information centre has seen a 200 per cent increase in inquiries since promotion. 'The club's success has given us an extra boost,' said Ann Untisz, a tourism officer. 'People have heard of us now and we have a higher profile.'

While most visiting supporters will see just Oakwell, others will choose to spend the weekend in Barnsley. They will discover that 10 per cent of the borough is in the Peak District National Park and that 70 per cent of it is designated green belt. There are country homes, museums, art galleries, country parks, monuments, walled gardens, steam railways and markets. Cicero has the county of Cumbria as a client and, should Barnsley call, it is ready for the challenge. 'I think changing Barnsley's image would have to be done gradually. There is too much history to shrug off in a short space of time,' said Stringer. 'It would be no use overdoing it and trying to fool people that Barnsley is something that it isn't. We couldn't say that everything is rosy in the garden when people remember miners scrapping with policemen at the pit gates just a few years ago.'

Any marketing sheen placed on Barnsley should not be allowed to camouflage the truth. The place is beset by economic problems and a new report has claimed that it is the poorest town in Britain. A glimpse through the local newspaper, the *Barnsley Chronicle*, reveals a panoply of social problems. The role of dishonour includes the usual small-town amalgam of drug-dealers, drunks, aggressors, racists, television licence dodgers and people who relieve themselves in hedgerows after a night on the tiles.

The football club has done much to ameliorate the town's sullied image, both through its success and its enterprising style of play, but this week it was drawn into ignominy when Dean Jones, a 20-year-old reserve team player, failed a drug test. He has the woeful distinction of being the first player at a Premiership club to do so. Jones, who was born in Barnsley and still lives in the town, tested positive for amphetamine and could face a suspension. He has never played for the first team, or indeed been in a first-team squad. In recent weeks he has also struggled to make the reserves. No matter; the incident has brought shame on the club. 'He was tested on a Monday morning and the feeling locally is that he had taken something over the weekend, perhaps on a Saturday night and it was still in his system,' said an insider.

It is widely accepted that each generation has its own particular palate for the use of intoxicants and Jones, if his drug-taking is proved to be solely recreational, is far from atypical. The difference is that he is a professional footballer with Barnsley FC, and Barnsley, the town and the club, can do without yet another slur on its good name, however it is pronounced.

---

*Saturday 22 November 1997*

### Liverpool 0 Barnsley 1

Barnsley were expected to suffer another comprehensive defeat but held on for a win. The goal was scored by Ashley Ward who had recovered from his brief illness. It was only Barnsley's second win in the previous 11 league matches. A true reflection of the play would have been a comfortable victory for Liverpool.

Peter Markstedt, a new signing from SK Vasteraas of Sweden, made his début in defence after joining Barnsley just a few days earlier. His team-mates spotted his ear-ring and he was dubbed immediately 'Another Mary Appleby', the term of endearment for Matty Appleby, their long-haired team-mate.

The editors of the Liverpool match programme proved themselves masters of tact by including the paragraph: 'Barnsley have conceded 18 goals in three games against Arsenal, Chelsea and Manchester United alone and a staggering 40 in 15 games so far, which puts them firmly on course to beat the Premiership record of 100 conceded by Swindon in their one and only season in 1993-94.' In fact, Barnsley conceded 82 goals during their season in the Premiership, none of them at Anfield.

After the game, a youth threw a stone at the coach carrying the Barnsley squad as it made its way through heavy traffic on the outskirts of Liverpool. A side panel was smashed but no-one was hurt. Police gave chase and caught him in a side-street.

---

A MIRACLE ON MERSEYSIDE
*(The Times, Saturday 29 November 1997)*

The ball is in the net (apparently), and my new best friend has me in an aggressively affectionate headlock. He is screaming, yelling, shouting down my ear. When my Brother Grim finally lets go, I have to stay on my feet and volunteer an extra syllable to Barnsley as we cheer 'Barns-a-lee' to the afternoon sky.

I am not a Barnsley supporter (I am not even from Yorkshire), yet here I am at Anfield, the only impartial observer among 3,000 devotees in the away end. As experiences go, this is strictly X-Files, like passing a church and suddenly finding yourself at a wedding ceremony among strangers, and strange strangers at that.

The day begins at Oakwell, a fog drifting across the club car park. We all have neatly printed coach tickets and neatly packed lunches. Barnsley, at the foot of the table, have lost their past five away games and conceded 40 goals already this season. Understandably, no-one mentions football as the coach picks its way through the mist towards Liverpool. The man behind me, however, mentions crisps a lot. He has a two-year-old grandson and has found a sure-fire way of making baby-sitting easy. 'Crisps, I just feed him crisps,' he explains. 'How many does tha' give him?' asks his friend. 'Oh, about four packets.'

The coach pulls up alongside Stanley Park at the ludicrously early time of 1.30 pm; it is going to be a long day. I look at my match ticket and start to worry: Row 1, Seat 36, and, just to confirm that I have got the seat from hell, stamped across it is 'Uncovered Seat', which means: get set to get wet. Now, I'm actually very lucky to have the ticket at all. Barnsley is a club loyal to its principles, and, initially, only season-ticket holders were allowed to buy one.'They'd lynch me if I sold one to a reporter,' revealed a member of staff.

Row 1, Seat 36, in the Lower Anfield Road End is as appalling as it sounds. To create Row 1, Seat 36 in your own living room, you must switch on *Match of the Day* and lie down flat on your stomach about six inches from the television. Place a fruit bowl between you and the screen – at Anfield, this is a photographer and his equipment – and, just in case there remains a modicum of enjoyment from your mole's eye-view, ask various members of your family to push past wearing fluorescent jackets in the manner of club stewards.

The supporters sharing my mole hole all appear to be disconcertingly above average height and weight, not to mention volume and intoxication. On either side sit two blokes the size of telephone boxes. When they both stand up, which is every ten seconds, I have no choice but to rise with them. The one on my left is middle-aged, and, it seems, fairly peaceable. Abruptly, he asks a steward to move out of the way. 'You couldn't organise a piss-up in a brewery, yer Scouse bastard,' he yells as an afterthought. If football has gone effete, no one has told Barnsley. Everyone sings. Mums, dads, lads, they all scream themselves hoarse, and the look in their eyes is intense; it betrays a raw, bloody-minded passion for their team, their town, their family, their mates. They sing as if their lives depend on it, and I do too.

Out on the pitch, Barnsley are hardly in the game, but, on a break, the ball appears to find its way into Liverpool's net. Here comes my head lock, and, for a horrible second, my neighbour is squeezing me violently, pressing his face close to mine. In this mêlée of hostile pleasure, I have never felt so lonely, never missed my own team and my own kind so much. No-one in the stalls has any idea who has scored, since the goal went in at the Kop End, which is only visible with the aid of a tripod and a pair of binoculars. Somehow, Barnsley hold out and the goal celebrations are repeated at the end of the match. They are given extra seasoning as the supporters around me goad the stewards and police into a few minor skirmishes.

Back on the coach, we are made to wait an hour before setting off, and it takes almost another hour to negotiate the traffic congestion in Liverpool. It is still foggy in Barnsley when we arrive just before 8 pm. A couple are leaving their house, dressed up for a Saturday night out. 'Was it a good match?' they shout. 'Yeah,' I reply instinctively. The truth is, I don't know.

---

While the fiasco of my day out at Anfield made good copy, it was an example of the club's heedless PR. When I first asked to buy a ticket, I received a definite refusal. At great lengths, I was told how unfair it would be that a Barnsley supporter would miss out on the seat I was occupying. I accepted the point, and admired it to a degree, but had the feeling that they were making too much fuss over the issue. Most fans accept that sacrifices have to be made sometimes for the greater good of the club. It is open to debate, but to lose one seat out of more than 3,000 in exchange for a 1,000-word article in a national newspaper would seem a reasonable swap.

The club compounded matters by contacting me at the eleventh hour and informing me that I could, after all, have a ticket. I was told repeatedly that I was fortunate to receive it, but, after attending the game, I now believe it was one that they simply had not sold, rather than one that they had reserved specially. I had to pay for the ticket, which I did not mind, though this seemed petty in the light of all the coverage, almost all of it positive, I had garnered for the club.

The seat, on the front row, was just as described in the article. It is an insult for Liverpool to charge supporters (who are not privy to the vagaries of Anfield's vantage points) so much to witness no more than a blur of ankles and shin pads. It was also insulting that Barnsley should consider it magnanimous on their behalf to put me in such a seat. It had 'uncovered' stamped across it, and Row 1 would tend to suggest the view would be mainly of the perimeter fence and a few photographers. How do Barnsley treat their enemies?

After the piece appeared, I received criticism for giving the Barnsley supporters 'a bad name'. Again, this was partly the fault of the club. There had clearly been some demarcation in the allocation of tickets. I would guess that they had gone on sale to the different classifications of supporters, on a definite strata system from the top to the bottom of the Anfield Road end. The best seats had been sold to established season-ticket holders, while the front-row tickets had been on open sale. The sole representative of the press, therefore, was unwisely placed among what the club considered its lowest class of supporter.

I chose to write a humorous piece, but it could easily have been a damning indictment of the Barnsley support, if not the club itself. Those nearest to me were some of the worst behaved supporters I have been among. They hardly watched the match, and spent most of the time wandering around, waving to their friends, chatting, or looking for the toilets. I did not speak to anyone because there was a real sense of regional allegiance and I heard a few Barnsley supporters 'challenged' because they did not speak in a broad South Yorkshire accent. 'I live in London now, but I'm from Barnsley originally, like' they would say.

*Saturday 29 November 1997*

**Barnsley 2 Leeds United 3**

A two-goal lead within the first 20 minutes, courtesy of Ashley Ward and Andy Liddell, should have set Barnsley on course for victory but Leeds hit back with goals by Alf-Inge Haarland and Rod Wallace before substitute Derek Lilley scored a late winner for the visitors.

Barnsley fans found themselves lampooned in a Leeds fanzine that claimed their staple diet was tap water and salted pieces of coal and that voters had put the town on the map by electing a whippet as an MP.

CHAPTER FIVE

A Nation Apart

## Redfearn Basks In Limelight Of Centre Stage
### (*The Times, Saturday 6 December 1997*)

Successful footballers have their own particular accessories and Neil Redfearn, the Barnsley captain, is no exception as he drives into the hotel car park in a BMW, wearing a baseball cap and, for good measure, with his agent in tow. For a few rueful seconds, he looks the identikit Premiership footballer, set to proffer a few words of anodyne wisdom in exchange for discreet mentions for the sponsors of his tracksuit, boots or haircut. About as discreet as a Roy Keane tackle, that is.

He winds down the car window and beams a smile warm enough to melt the frost smattered across the hotel grounds. 'All right, lads?' he says in a dense Yorkshire accent. 'I won't be a minute, I'll just park my car.' When they come to make the rags to riches, Hartlepool to Arsenal, Gow to Di Matteo biopic of Redfearn, American audiences will need subtitles. Our photographer senses Redfearn's congenial nature and suggests a few shots before the interview. Normally, this request comes after some banal, sycophantic chat, during which time the subject is sufficiently softened up for a trial by camera. 'No problem,' says Redfearn, and sits down on the cold hard steps outside the hotel. He does not ask that we photograph his good side, or indeed his sponsored side.

His agent is a sweet, middle-aged lady called Margaret. 'I've just come to make sure everything is all right,' she says. There is no talk of fees or copy approval, it is all commendably informal. Plates of mince pies are brought before us and Redfearn hands her a bundle of mail. 'She's great, is Margaret. She's my press agent really,' he said. 'I get loads of mail each week and she helps sort it all out. It's amazing how much I get now we're in the Premiership.'

Redfearn, at 32, has taken 17 years, eight clubs and more than 600 matches to reach football's top table. He is the ultimate football journeyman; a reliable, intelligent playmaker with a thunderous shot and a penchant for scoring spectacular goals. Earlier in the season Barnsley played Chelsea at Oakwell and Redfearn was singled out by Di Matteo. 'He was telling me what he was going to do to me and I had to laugh really. I've been to places like Hartlepool where there used to be holes in the dressing-room walls and I've played in games where someone's battered me from one end of the pitch to the other for 90 minutes,' he said.

He started his career at Nottingham Forest but was homesick and returned to the North with Bolton Wanderers, for whom he made his début in 1982 against Rotherham United. 'I'll never forget that match,' he said. 'I accidentally kicked Gerry Gow of all people and he said to me, "Do that again and I'll break your nose!"' His father, Brian, had also been a professional footballer, turning out as a winger for a clutch of Northern lower-league teams and it looked for a while as if Neil would emulate him, as he joined Lincoln City and Doncaster Rovers. 'We used to have to ring the bank at Doncaster and make sure we'd been paid. It upsets me to see that they are in trouble again at the moment,' he said. 'I think it is important to the game that smaller clubs survive.'

Although, by his own admission, he is short of pace, Redfearn reached a higher level with Crystal Palace and Watford and, in 1989, was an integral part of the enterprising Oldham Athletic team built by Joe Royle. He played in the centre of midfield during Oldham's promotion to the top flight in 1990-91 and scored 14 league goals. The summer of 1991 in Oldham was much like the summer of 1997 in Barnsley. Camera crews descended on an allegedly grim Northern town and the euphoria was intense. During that close season, Royle had a quiet but devastating word with Redfearn. 'He told me he wanted to play me on the right of midfield,' recalled Redfearn. 'I felt I'd more than earned the right to play in my own position. I'd always seen Joe like a father figure, but it felt like he had kicked me in the teeth.' After taking Oldham to the top, Redfearn was to play no part in their glory and left to join Barnsley, who were then bottom of the old Second Division with just one point from seven games. 'It meant a lot to me to play for a Yorkshire club. I felt I could relate to their supporters,' he said.

Last season, Barnsley played joyous, unfettered football and their promotion was greeted by universal acclaim. 'We had no fear at all. If we went 3-0 down, we just assumed we'd come back and score four,' Redfearn said. 'When we came up it was like a shot in the arm for the working man and I think most people want us to stay up.' Unfortunately, Barnsley's progressive football has not been a success in the Premiership. Their defence has remained generous, but this has not been reciprocated by opponents. The philosophy of optimism instilled by Danny Wilson has not perished entirely, however. 'Even when we were seven goals down against Manchester United the other week I kept thinking, if we could get a goal or two we might have a mini-revival and make it 7-4 or something,' said Redfearn.

Redfearn is steeped in football. He has been coached professionally since the age of seven. Talking about the game comes as naturally as playing it. He is interrupted several times by hotel staff tendering opinions on Barnsley's struggle. He looks them in the eye, listens to their comments and counters with his own. As we leave, after all this free, unguarded conversation, he delivers a sting – except it is not really a sting at all. 'Margaret reckons I'd be good on things like *A Question of Sport* and doing stuff like this all helps, I suppose,' he says. A question of integrity would be just as appropriate.

---

*Monday 8 December 1997*

## Sheffield Wednesday 2 Barnsley 1

Before the game, few will have noted the identity of the referee. Afterwards, the Barnsley supporters would never again forget the name Gary Willard, for he was to play a great part in their fortunes.

Sheffield Wednesday took the lead through Dejan Stefanovic but Neil Redfearn equalised before half-time direct from a free kick on the edge of the penalty area. Paolo Di Canio,

Wednesday's tempestuous striker, was booked for fouling Darren Barnard and remained on the pitch despite a constant dialogue with the match officials. In the final minute he picked up a poor clearance, side-stepped Lars Leese, and secured the win. After three weeks in second-from-bottom place, the defeat consigned Barnsley to the foot of the table, where they were to remain for 10 weeks.

Barnsley fans were outraged by the leniency shown to Di Canio. Malcolm Moyes, a supporter writing in the *Sheffield Star*'s 'Green 'Un', commented: 'I am baffled as to how Fowlo di Canio could boot the ball away, make a number of obvious gestures of contempt to the linesman and commit a tackle on Appleby which should have got him a two-year prison sentence, and still be on the field to score a sickening winner.'

---

LOOK BACK TO WORLD OF DIFFERENCE
*(The Times, Saturday 13 December 1997)*

We expect our sporting heroes to be immortal. They should live for ever in the moment of their glory – young, supremely fit, blithe, free from the stress that encumbers an everyday life. Footballers, especially, are perceived as forever people, their huge wages sanctioning a life of eternal youth and opulence. When their careers are over, we do not expect to see them at the greengrocers or working in a factory. In our dreams, they remain a race apart, young and glamorous, frozen in time.

John McCann is in the small kitchen of his house in Barnsley, quietly thumbing through the pages of his scrapbook, stopping occasionally to linger over a photograph. There are two John McCanns present. One is 63 and recently made redundant after 26 years in a carpet factory. The other, staring out from a picture, is a handsome, dark-haired professional footballer, sweeping past defenders, the crowd roaring at his back. 'That's me playing at Charlton,' he says. He comes across a team photograph of Barnsley in 1957 – young men, arms crossed, ready to do battle. 'Four of that team are dead now," he says, and starts to run through a depressing roll call. 'Bobby Wood had a bad stroke and died ...' There is, thankfully, one success story. 'The big lad at the back, Duncan [Sharp], has done all right for himself. He has got his own haulage company,' said McCann.

In the old pictures, there is the inventory of football – the kits, players, crowd, an earnest pursuit of the ball – but the game and the lifestyle it perpetuates has since transmogrified. McCann talks about the modern game, but it is clear that it is beyond his ken and reach. 'It has changed drastically since I played,' he said. 'I used to be a ball player, but it is all one touch now and so quick. Most of the players comfortable on the ball are foreigners.'

McCann began his career as a winger with Bridgeton Waverley, a Scottish junior side. He was working as a trainee manager at his local Co-op when Barnsley offered him a professional contract for £17 per week. He left his home city of Glasgow and arrived in Yorkshire in December 1955, lodging with an elderly couple. There was no gymnasium at Oakwell, so training sessions took place outside. They trained whatever the weather and he cannot recall a single cancellation. During the pre-season, players took part in 'fast walking', trudging through the streets of Barnsley in the July sunshine. 'We used to do five or six miles. They always found us plenty of hills,' recalled McCann. 'I remember one, Hound Hill. Oh God, I can see it now.'

McCann found the club an extremely hierarchical structure and though he sometimes used to see the chairman, Joe Richards, and the board of directors, the players considered these men in overcoats to be 'like gods'. After four years at Oakwell, he was told by one of these 'gods' that a transfer to Bristol City had been arranged. He was sold for £21,000, a handsome profit on Barnsley's initial investment of less than £1,000.

The training at Bristol was eccentric. In practice matches, McCann often found that there was no opposition. They would merely run forward, pass the ball between themselves and score goals at will. 'It was silly. I thought, "God almighty, what's this in aid of?"' he said. In a facetious mood one morning, he deliberately kicked the ball out of play, knowing this would effectively end the game because there was no opponent to take the throw-in. 'I was sent for an early bath and I never made the first team again after that,' he said.

He moved on and later played for Derby County, Huddersfield Town and Chesterfield before returning to Barnsley to set up a business with his brother-in-law as a panel beater and sprayer. The venture did not materialise, so McCann took a job at Shaw Carpets in Barnsley, where he remained until his redundancy. 'It was strange doing an ordinary job to begin with, but it became all right,' he said. Surprisingly, despite living a mile from Oakwell, he has not been back since the day that he was transferred. He was playing golf when they clinched promotion to the Premiership last April. He says he is 'happy' that they have done so well, but his sense of detachment from it all is extraordinary.

His wife, Eileen, returns and while her husband has his picture taken in another room she talks about life as a footballer's wife. She does not mention glory, wealth or kudos, but remembers 'standing outside in the pouring rain after matches, not even offered a cup of tea'. She rues that players were not given any help for a life after football. Suddenly, she asks why anyone is interested in him after all this time. It would take too long to explain.

---

*Saturday 13 December 1997*

### Barnsley 2 Newcastle United 2

An exquisite goal by substitute John Hendrie against his former club earned Barnsley a deserved draw in a thrilling match. Keith Gillespie (two) scored for Newcastle, while Neil Redfearn notched Barnsley's other goal.

---

*Monday 15 December 1997*

The Barnsley squad had their annual Christmas trawl around the town's pubs and clubs. Most wore fancy dress, including Lars Leese in national costume of lederhosen and hiking boots, Neil Thompson as Adolf Hitler, and Darren Sheridan as the lead character from the film, *The Mask*. A highlight of the evening was a karaoke session when Adie Moses and Darren Barnard ran through 'Jumping Jack Flash'.

---

*Friday 19 December 1997*

My request for an interview with Dean Jones was turned down by Danny Wilson. He wrote: 'Unfortunately it is not appropriate at the present time, he still has a hearing with the FA to consider very soon and we don't want anything to jeopardise that. Thank you for your understanding in this matter.'

---

HENDRIE PLAYS FOR LAUGHS
*(The Times, Saturday 20 December 1997)*

A mention of his name is enough to inspire unfeasibly wide smiles. There will then follow a story, some improbable tale of mischief involving shaving foam or a hotel minibar. Everyone in football seems to have a John Hendrie story; he is an anecdote in football boots.

Two of the more recent tales make revealing bookends to his personality. His German team-mate, Lars Leese, was being interviewed by a journalist at Oakwell when, out in the corridor, Hendrie could be heard goose-stepping and singing war songs. If he is big on laughs, he is also big on heart. Last week, without telling anyone at the club, or the media, he attended a primary school in Stokesley, near Middlesbrough, where three children have died (in separate, unrelated circumstances) within the past year or so. He gave a reading and lifted spirits significantly.

Hendrie has just published *Don't Call Me Happy!*, a breezy resume of a life in football that has included a free transfer at 20, the emotional trauma of the Bradford fire disaster, seven different clubs, almost 500 league matches and nearly as many pranks. While the book reinforces the belief that professional footballers have much in common with a bunch of giddy 14-year-olds on an outward bound course, it also offers a remarkable insight. He has managed to distil a personality that is lively and candid into its 200 pages. He admires the professionalism of Howard Wilkinson, for example, but thinks he is 'devoid of humour'. He is similarly diplomatic when describing Carlton Palmer, whose own mastery of tact ran to abusing Hendrie in the players' lounge while he was talking to a nun and a 77-year-old neighbour. 'He showed a lack of professionalism and maturity,' Hendrie understates.

'I'm known in the game as a bit of a joker, so I suppose that's where a lot of the book is coming from. I used to be pretty intense when I was a younger player but I've mellowed out now,' he said. His reputation precedes him, so, when he is an hour late for the interview, and a note is thrust into my hands by the hotel staff, trepidation reigns. 'Mr Hendry [sic] will arrive soon,' it reads. Whether he will arrive dressed as a window cleaner or in his pyjamas is another matter. Eventually, he shows, and the attire is unmistakably footballer – a bulky nylon coat emblazoned with logos, a pair of jeans and just-washed hair. It was a close call, though, he had spent the previous day as a 'Scouser', cruising the Barnsley night-spots in a violet shell suit with the rest of the Barnsley squad on their annual Christmas get-together.

'We were going to have a bad-taste pub crawl at first. We were all going to go as Georgi Hristov!' he said. Hristov, the club's Macedonian striker, has arrived in South Yorkshire with an abundance of polo-necked sweaters and tank tops that have generated much mirth. The mood in the Barnsley camp has remained high, despite their position at the bottom of the Premiership. 'Our heads are not down, the spirit is really high. Danny Wilson is a good motivator and has worked hard to make sure we have remained positive,' he said.

The last time Hendrie encountered a similar spirit was during his six seasons with Middlesbrough. It was eventually destroyed by the arrival of Ravanelli *et al*. In the book, he provides a fascinating snapshot of life in the Middlesbrough dressing-room during its famously cosmopolitan period. In short, Juninho was 'one of the lads' and respected by all, while Ravanelli was a 'very selfish guy who cared nothing about team spirit'. He describes an incident when Ravanelli was shaking everyone's hand before taking to the pitch. When he came to Hendrie, who was a substitute, he ignored him. 'He clearly believed shaking hands with someone who wasn't even in the team was beneath him. He walked by me as if I was nothing,' said Hendrie.

It would appear that much of the media supposition about Middlesbrough at the time was authentic. The foreign players were habitually late for training and did not honour curfews; this, inevitably, had a divisive effect. After a home defeat against Arsenal, Juninho and Ravanelli were practically fighting with one another, with various interpreters explaining to the others that the Italian accused the Brazilian of being 'greedy', while the retort was that Ravanelli was 'jealous'.

Moving to Barnsley allowed Hendrie to remain in Yorkshire, where he had settled with his wife, Linda, after joining Bradford City in 1984. 'Danny Wilson sold Barnsley to me really well. He told me that they had a real chance of promotion,' he said. Promotion was duly achieved last April, though the moment was tinged by some sadness because it was secured against his former club, Bradford, who were thrown deeper into a relegation struggle.

Barnsley take on Tottenham Hotspur today in another relegation match. Hendrie is not sure whether he will make the team or once more grace the substitutes' bench. Either way, the smile will remain.

———————

# A RACE APART

*Saturday 20 December 1997*

## Tottenham Hotspur 3 Barnsley 0

Gerry Francis, the former England captain, had resigned as manager at Tottenham Hotspur and was replaced by Christian Gross. Barnsley, once more, showed little fight and lost ground to another team in poor form. Allan Nielsen and David Ginola (two) scored their goals, which all came within the first 18 minutes.

Once again, Danny Wilson was furious. 'Our defending was absolutely pathetic, and our game plan went out of the window in the first five minutes because players were not doing their jobs,' he said.

Barnsley, stuck at the foot of the table, had won just four league games in their first 19 matches and conceded 50 goals. Many predicted that they would finish the season conceding more goals than any other team in the history of the Premiership.

*Monday 22 December 1997*

Dean Jones appeared before the FA and was banned from playing for three months. He told the hearing that he had taken the drugs in a nightclub to help him stay awake in the early hours. He admitted he had been 'very foolish'. The club promised to stand by the player. 'Until this incident he had been a model professional and he is full of remorse,' said Michael Spinks.

*Friday 26 December 1997*

## Bolton Wanderers 1 Barnsley 1

Relegation rivals Bolton were outplayed in the first half and Barnsley should have had more for their efforts than a solitary Georgi Hristov goal. Bolton rallied after the interval and secured a draw with a magnificent shot by their captain, Gudni Bergsson.

---

### BARNSLEY'S DISCARDED HERO HAS NO REGRETS
*(The Times, Saturday 27 December 1997)*

The ball was punted through the drizzle towards Bradford City's penalty area. Amid a battery of elbows and knees jostling for kicking space, Paul Wilkinson volunteered his forehead. The ball ricocheted beyond the goalkeeper, Aidan Davison, and sailed into the net.

At 3.21 pm on Saturday 26 April 1997, Wilkinson found himself at the epicentre of British football. His goal had set Barnsley on course for promotion to football's top flight after a 110-year wait. Hundreds had worn the Barnsley shirt before him, but he was the chosen man. After the match, the players, with their wives and girlfriends, celebrated long into the night and Wilkinson was feted at every turn. He was bought enough drinks to last another 110 years and his fiancée had to step aside while appreciative fans planted beery kisses on his cheeks. 'Thank you, thank you,' they blubbered, and swore their everlasting love.

Sentimentality is an indulgence afforded to football supporters. We reminisce, rue and romanticise until, eventually, even 4-0 home defeats take on a charm of their own. Unfortunately, football clubs are not privy to this convention, as Wilkinson soon discovered. As he punched the air and danced across the turf, he was not to know that it would be his final full appearance at Oakwell in a Barnsley shirt. In one photograph of the after-match celebrations, he was pictured kissing his shirt. He was not to know it was a good-bye kiss.

He had played in all but one of Barnsley's games in the First Division, but fell foul of the paradox that, by lifting the club to a higher status, he also lifted himself out of a job. The wealth generated by promotion enabled Danny Wilson to purchase Georgi Hristov from Partizan Belgrade and, a few weeks into the campaign, Ashley Ward from Derby County.

Just five months after his moment of glory, Wilkinson was collecting his boots from Oakwell and heading to London where he joined Millwall in a £150,000 deal. The Barnsley supporters had promised him the world, while the club balked at the two-year contract he felt he deserved. 'It can be a harsh world, but ultimately we accept as footballers that we are commodities. I had become surplus to requirements at Barnsley,' he said.

He had joined Barnsley on a free transfer from Middlesbrough, where he had spent four seasons. He was reunited with his former Middlesbrough strike partner, John Hendrie. They formed a potent combination, and scored 114 goals between them in five seasons together. 'I was struck with Barnsley straight away. It is a homely club but it has a lot of ambition. There was a real buzz about the town,' said Wilkinson. He felt this energy at close quarters, living in Cawthorne, on the outskirts of the town.

While Barnsley's trademark last season was thoughtful, passing football, Wilkinson felt his role was more rudimentary. 'It was a real pass-and-move team, but I gave them another dimension. I was the tallest, and since I'm not the most skilful player in the world, they tended to use me more as a battering ram and play off me,' he said.

At Christmas last year, Barnsley had lost just three times in 23 league matches. They have won just four games in 20 this season and have conceded 51 league goals already. Few Barnsley fans expected anything but a fraught battle for survival, but, inevitably, there have been a few grumbles muttered into the beers.

Some feel that Wilson tinkered needlessly with the winning team. 'I think Danny should have given last year's team longer to come good, but I'm bound to think that, aren't I?' said Wilkinson. 'I have no hard feelings towards him or Barnsley, I always look for their score first.'

Wilkinson's final appearance for Barnsley was against Chelsea when they were beaten 6-0 in August. He was substituted at half-time and had a spectator's view of the second-half annihilation. 'I think they've learnt a lot since then and have adapted well. There is no problem at Barnsley because no-one expected them to survive anyway,' he says. 'I've a sneaking feeling, though, that they are going to stay up. I don't think people appreciate the spirit and resolve within the club.'

Instead of a season at football's top table, Wilkinson is among the blood and thud of the journeymen of the Nationwide Second Division. He suffered a 'whack on the ankle' last Saturday in Millwall's win against Wycombe Wanderers and has spent most of this week under treatment. 'It's a lot more physical than I expected,' he said. He cannot complain too volubly since Billy Bonds, the Millwall manager, signed him chiefly because he remembered fractious encounters when he was a defender with West Ham United and Wilkinson played for Nottingham Forest. 'I left him with six stitches in his forehead after one match, and he still signed me,' said Wilkinson.

He has moved with his fiancée to Bromley, Kent, and, though he recalls his time at Barnsley fondly, he has no qualms about swapping clubs for the seventh time in his career, at the age of 33. 'I would have loved to have stayed there for another couple of seasons, but that's not what I was offered,' he said. 'That's just the way it is in football.'

---

*Sunday 28 December 1997*

### Barnsley 1 Derby County 0

Ashley Ward scored against his former club and kept Barnsley within catching distance of Bolton and Crystal Palace at the foot of the table. Derby had their share of the play, but Barnsley defended well.

WEST STAND
UPPER TIER
BLOCKS C, D & E
HOME SUPPORTERS
TICKET HOLDERS ONLY

29                29

CHAPTER SIX

Going on a Bear Hunt

## SILENT REVOLUTION BREEDS RESOLUTION
*(The Times, Saturday 3 January 1998)*

A revolution is under way in Barnsley. Across the town, from Smithies to Worsbrough, Darton to Grimethorpe, they are calling time on the trend of giving fey and fanciful names to pubs. The Rose and Thistle became Silvers and then, a year or so later, the Tut 'n' Shive. Meanwhile, regulars found themselves transported from the Magnet to Dolly's to the Beer Emporium without ever actually swapping their local. 'Some of the changes are absolutely ludicrous,' complained Harold Hackney, the town's licensing chairman. Around these parts, change has to be made with the soft brush of discretion. Too much clamour and the murmur becomes a moan becomes a mutiny. There remains a sense of clanship, born from a mining ancestry where life or death literally depended on the actions of peers.

Within the town, there has been much dewy-eyed sentimentality focused on Barnsley's promotion. A limited run of commemorative promotion tankards was advertised before Christmas. It was another conspicuous attempt to freeze the recent past. The date when promotion was clinched – 26 April 1997 – has become a jewel of nostalgia, caressed and admired like a piece of family silver. Amid all this cosy reminiscing, the roof has started to leak and no-one, thus far, has bothered to do much about it.

Only now, five months into their Premiership campaign, has change been fomented. 'We want to be more like Wimbledon,' declared Neil Redfearn, the club captain, last week. Basically, this means Barnsley are a pub name-change in reverse; where they were once Dolly's, they are now the Rose and Thistle. Fey and fanciful football has been superseded by the linear and combative. Statistics show that much of Barnsley's play this season has been on the offensive. They have, for example, won more corners than Manchester United and had players caught offside more frequently than Arsenal. While they have held territory, their naiveté has allowed opponents, within a space of a few astute passes, to zip the ball into their net, often with humiliating ease.

Over the Christmas period, a draw away to Bolton Wanderers (whom they play in the FA Cup today) and a win against Derby County brought Barnsley four points. In both games, there were perceptible signs of a new maturity. Extra bodies were placed in midfield and the team's natural flair was tempered by caution and an admirable work-rate. These are the primary attributes of the survivor, if not the entertainer. A squad system is also developing at Oakwell, where there is a queue of eager foot-soldiers willing to run themselves into dust. Sheridan will make way for Tinkler who will make way for Bullock; it will depend on whether the job requires a strategy that is, respectively, holding, man-on-man or quixotic. Earlier in the season, Barnsley regularly fell into apoplexy when surrounded by stars from football's elite. Players like Vialli, Cole and Bergkamp were allowed to race past and the only anxiety of the Barnsley team was that, back home, no-one had pressed the record button on the video to frame them next to these comets.

Their victory at Anfield in November, though fortuitous, roused an assurance that they were worthy of a place among football's hierarchy. One local paper issued a special badge with the aphorism 'Liverpool Kopped It'. While it was intended as a piece of fun, it hinted at the parochialism that has sometimes undermined Barnsley. The win was remarkable, but it was not an *achievement*.

The running-down of the coal industry in Barnsley has left a legacy of mistrust of government and police. Sometimes the net widens to include any figure of authority or outsider. When the Barnsley supporters sing about the republic of South Yorkshire, there is not a trace of irony. They appear to take a perverse joy in viewing themselves as the forgotten, the wronged. A report just published reveals that Barnsley is near the bottom of the UK's life-expectancy 'league'. This news was reported locally in an almost gleeful 'told-you-so' manner, as if there was kudos in suffering. Danny Wilson has learnt to harness this powerful negative energy. After his team was disparaged by Mark McGhee, the Wolverhampton Wanderers manager, he pinned up his comments in the dressing-room. This season there is a new Lucifer. Mark Lawrenson might be a composed, perceptive pundit to most of the nation, but to a Barnsley fan he carries a three-pronged fork and a pitcher of molten lava. 'I hope Barnsley enjoy the Premiership, because next season I'm afraid they'll be back in the Nationwide League,' was his transgression on *Match of the Day*. Now, whenever Barnsley nudge ahead of their opponents in a match, supporters sing to the television cameras: 'Are you watching, Lawrenson?'

As we draw slowly into 1998, Barnsley's fight for survival is at its halfway stage. Despite their league position, optimism still triumphs. The demon in their midst might well form a crucial addition.

---

*Saturday 3 January 1998*

### Barnsley 1 Bolton Wanderers 0
### (FA Cup Third Round)

A quickly-taken free kick by Darren Barnard set Barnsley on their way to a memorable cup run. Neil Redfearn had intended to take the kick, but Barnard stepped in while the defensive wall was being assembled.

The game was marred by a scuffle on the touchline where several punches were thrown. A steward was arrested but later released without being charged.

Afterwards, newspapers made reference to an incident between Neil Cox, the Bolton defender, and a 'ball boy' who refused to retrieve the ball. The 'ball boy' was Eric Winstanley, the Barnsley first-team coach, aged 53.

---

*Tuesday 6 January 1998*

A news story broke that Georgi Hristov had labelled Barnsley women 'ugly' and that they drank too much alcohol. The media used the story to take a swipe at Barnsley and reinforce its downbeat image.

------------

*Thursday 8 January 1998*

The club called a press conference at Oakwell to refute the allegations supposedly made by Hristov. 'It was a scurrilous, mischievous piece of journalism,' said Danny Wilson.

Ivan Ridulovic of the Belgrade-based newspaper, *Civa Politica*, had conducted the original interview and confirmed that Hristov was misquoted by an irresponsible news agency that had picked up on his original story. For the record, Hristov had said he was homesick and that women in Barnsley drank alcohol, which he was not used to. Women back home in Macedonia were teetotal because of their religious beliefs.

Sue Markham of the Barnsley Supporters' Club was happy to forgive and forget, as she embraced Hristov for the benefit of the press. 'I never believed it. Georgi is too nice and polite to say anything like that,' she cooed.

------------

### Banging The Drum For Barnsley
*(The Times, Saturday 10 January 1998)*

The Beach Boys, the Monkees and Aretha Franklin are among the phalanx of pop legends on an album that forms the musical accompaniment to some serious cutting of the rug. Tucked in between Rod Stewart and the Spice Girls on the succinctly titled CD, *The Best Party Album In The World ... Ever*, is the Yorkshire band, Chumbawamba, with 'Tubthumping'. If it seems a mite unlikely, the band's drummer, Harry Hamer, feels the same when he looks at the Premiership table. 'Just to see Barnsley up there, playing teams like Manchester United. I still can't believe it.' explained Hamer, a lifelong Barnsley supporter.

Chumbawamba are the Barnsley of the music scene. During their 16-year, nine-album career, they have been viewed as unfashionable, grouchy Northerners; rugged journeymen rather than silky playmakers. The boys (and three girls) done well, though. 'Tubthumping' has sold more than 750,000 copies in the United Kingdom alone and their latest album has nestled in the top ten in the United States for several weeks, selling two million copies in the process. In football terms, this is a 2-0 win at Old Trafford with United praying for the final whistle.

The qualities that have taken Barnsley to the Premiership are also distilled in Chumbawamba, who still boast six members from their original line-up. 'We've never had money thrown at us. We've got to where we are because we have worked hard and had a belief in ourselves. We've always worked as a team,' said Hamer.

Although he co-wrote 'Tubthumping', Hamer did not realise until afterwards that they had recorded the ultimate Barnsley theme tune. 'The lyrics could have been written specially for us,' said John Hendrie, the Barnsley striker. 'They sing, "O, Danny Boy, I get knocked down, but I get up again, you're never going to keep me down".' Although Leeds United have adopted it as their official theme song, it is played regularly in the Oakwell dressing-room. A hectic touring schedule has meant that Hamer has missed many Barnsley matches in recent years. On the day that promotion was sealed, he was listening to the radio on headphones while the band sound-checked for a concert in Ipswich. 'I was jumping up and down when I heard the score. I was really happy and I pulled on my Barnsley shirt for our encore,' he said.

He was first taken to Oakwell by his grandfather, Wilkinson Fearnley, a Barnsley devotee, in 1977, when Barnsley were in the old Fourth Division. 'I remember the noise and the ground looked really big, though it's not really. I was there with a silk scarf around my wrist, a denim jacket, the lot.'

He lived in the Barnsley district of Kendray and, later, Ardsley, and supporting Barnsley seemed an integral part of the local culture. Sometimes, such was his enthusiasm, he would arrive at the ground before the car-park attendants. 'There was a real routine to the weekend. You'd go to the Casa Disco record shop in town and buy a single on Saturday morning and then go to the match in the afternoon. On Sundays you'd go to your gran's for your dinner. I hate all this where all the young kids support Manchester United. It means so much more when it's your local club,' he said.

Chumbawamba had an extraordinary year in 1997. It began when their record company rejected tapes of their forthcoming album and advised them to take a year off. The band decided to swap labels and sign to EMI. After years of struggle, they were suddenly elevated to the status of household name. In America, they appeared on the David Letterman show, while in the UK they played the coveted New Year's Eve midnight spot on Channel 4's *TFI Friday*.

There was tangible, homespun proof of Chumbawamba's new standing when Harry's father, Jimmy Hamer, started to perform 'Tubthumping' as part of the cabaret act that he takes to all parts of Yorkshire under the stage name of Jimmy Echo. 'My dad also makes backing tapes for other singers and "Tubthumping" is his most popular of all time. I think "Lady in Red" is second and "Simply the Best" third. My parents weren't into me getting into music at first. It's weird how it's all turned out,' he said.

Hamer has bet money on Barnsley surviving in the Premiership, though he is philosophical about the prospects of relegation. 'I know that we're struggling, but we're there and if we go back down again, who cares? We've been in the Premier League. It's something my granddad would never have dreamt of. It's the same with the music, it was our year in 1997, but you don't know what's going to happen next,' he said.

Despite the new-found fame, the money due in royalties has not yet filtered through to the group, who still pay themselves £160 a week in wages and live in modest houses in Leeds. By all accounts, the royalties will be vast, not that Hamer plans to spend it heedlessly. Might he direct some of it towards his beloved Barnsley? 'Aye, I suppose we could sponsor the match ball or something, couldn't we?' he replied. And some.

———————

A few weeks after the interview Chumbawamba found themselves front page news when the group's Danbert Nobacon tipped water over the deputy prime minister, John Prescott, at the Brit Awards ceremony.

———————

*Saturday 10 January 1998*

**West Ham United 6 Barnsley 0**

A spineless display by Barnsley was punished by another six-goal drubbing. West Ham's goals were scored by Frank Lampard Jr, Amassi Abou (two), John Moncur, John Hartson and Stan Lazaridis. 'If we continue playing like this we will prove all the pundits right. We will be relegated,' said Wilson.

Chris Morgan made his début for Barnsley and was the only player excused the fury of Wilson. The young defender was hardly the team's lucky mascot. He had travelled with the squad to Arsenal where they were beaten 5-0 and Southampton where they lost 4-1; he was a non-playing substitute for the 4-1 defeat against Wimbledon, and then he finally came on to the field for the 6-0 defeat at Upton Park.

The West Ham game was Barnsley's last drubbing. Afterwards they did not lose by more than a two-goal margin in 21 league and cup games.

*Better Red Than Dead* highlighted the game as one of only a handful where the team had not shown the heart for the fight. 'To wave the white flag of apathy as we did against Southampton and West Ham is a betrayal of the dreams and aspirations of ordinary people whose lives are tied to the fortunes of their football team,' declared its editorial.

One Barnsley supporter unfurled a banner at the match reading: 'Georgi Is Innocent'. At half-time Hristov asked his team-mates what the word 'innocent' meant. He was told it was another word for ugly! The players had advised local girls to grow their armpit hair to a decent length if they wanted a date with Hristov, like the girls did in Macedonia.

# GOING ON A BEAR HUNT

## *Thursday 15 January 1998*

Jan-Aage Fjortoft joined Barnsley from Sheffield United for a fee of £850,000. The 31-year-old striker had played 70 times for Norway and was signed to bring some experience to the front-line. 'We had scoured the country, looking high and low for someone like him, and we have found him on our own doorstep,' said Wilson. He was immediately dubbed Jan-Aage Floorcloth by the Barnsley faithful.

---

## *Friday 16 January 1998*

Malcolm Shotton, reserve team coach, left the club to become manager at Oxford United. Shotton had been Wilson's first signing for Barnsley when he joined them as player/coach in July 1994. Peter Shirtliff, aged 36, who had not appeared in the first team since September, was appointed as Shotton's replacement.

---

## BARNSLEY AND THE MEDIA, THE END OF THE AFFAIR
### *(The Times, Saturday 17 January 1998)*

A smirk that radiates conceit falls immediately on to faces that were previously blank. 'A column on Barnsley called "Life At The Top"? Life at the bottom more like.' Hee, hee. Thereafter follows a joke, an old joke with a new, freshly-primed victim. 'Have you heard the one about the Barnsley goalkeeper?' We probably have, actually. Barnsley. Hold your sides, here it comes again – Barnsley. Just to say the word, preferably in an indolent Northern groan, is enough. Where, just a few months ago, it stood for romance, it now stands for ridicule. Barnsley, a nation's cherished underdog, has been disowned.

All the losing has simply got too much. A few narrow defeats and the odd 3-0 loss would not have been too bad, but to concede 57 goals in 22 games and rattle up so many 5-0, 6-0,

7-0 drubbings, is, well, embarrassing. West Ham United turned
them over last Saturday and Danny Wilson said it was his team's
worst performance of the season, and the competition is fierce.

The professional pundits, the Des Lynams and Gary
Linekers, have been at the vanguard of the scorn-mongering.
Look at their faces during the preamble to the screening of the
latest Barnsley calamity. There is either phoney solemnity that
borders on the comical, or a wistful patronising grin. Mark
Lawrenson at least had the integrity to say that he thought
Barnsley would be relegated; this is less hurtful than the
mischievous mockery of a raised eyebrow or a twitch of the lips.

When Barnsley were promoted to the Premiership they did
not seek eulogy. They were simply fulfilling a process that had
begun some years before. In short, they played good football,
won rather a lot of matches and, consequently, in the 1996-97
season, gained promotion. The song, the dance, the television
special and the parable was someone else's idea. For their part,
Barnsley were happy to oblige, it is in their nature. 'Interview
with Mr Wilson? Sure, step this way.' Naturally, they also wanted
to sell season tickets, and 110 years in the business of football
had taught them the importance of patting gift horses
affectionately on the saddle.

The club remained wonderfully stoic throughout a long hot
summer of media overindulgence. It does not have a designated
public relations department, so staff resorted to superannuated
virtues such as politeness when faced with a thousand and one
queries from reporters and producers. Cameras would linger
lovingly over bus stops, terraced houses and a redundant
pithead; at any minute someone might have even suggested a
musical. The media wanted desperately to sing this ballad of the
underdog. Barnsley had little say in the matter.

Barnsley are a typical example of a club adopted as a
statement or an addendum of personality. These passive
supporters will never be privy to the glorious intensity of
genuine partisanship. They fail to see that the connection
between a club and a supporter is from the heart, not the head.
Thousands championed Barnsley last year because they felt it

revealed themselves as warm-hearted and believers in dreams. That they should now eschew them is a testimony to their capricious and cynical nature. Long-term supporters have remained fiercely loyal. Their team might have suffered more heavy defeats than they expected, but they have viewed this season as a holiday, a metaphorical week in the sunshine after years of the humdrum. They are immensely forgiving and only an obvious lack of effort on the field draws forth serious reproach.

Last week, the female Barnsley contingent had their loyalty further tested when Georgi Hristov, the club's Macedonia striker, issued a broadside high on antagonism, low on subtlety. Barnsley women were ugly and drank too much beer, he claimed, allegedly. 'I did not say this,' pleaded Hristov at a hastily-arranged press conference. It appears that Hristov's original comments to a Belgrade news agency were far more benign, though it did not stop the British media enjoying a laugh at Barnsley's expense. This has understandably caused much consternation in the town and moved a local poet, Ian McMillan, to draft a piquant ode that closes with: ' ... and let's hope that soon the London press / will use another doorstop to drop their mess!'

Abandoned by their new-found fans, besmirched by the media, this is Barnsley's favourite tune. They rather enjoy the sense of isolation, a two-fingers-to-the-world stance. Not for them the broad, bland church of a Manchester United or Chelsea. This is about a district, a town, a community, a family, and everyone else can get lost. Or, get chuffing lost, as they say around here.

---

*Saturday 17 January 1998*

### Barnsley 1 Crystal Palace 0

The third consecutive 1-0 win at Oakwell saw Barnsley earn three points from fellow relegation strugglers, Crystal Palace.

Ashley Ward scored again, playing alongside his new striking partner, Fjortoft.

———————

*Saturday 24 January 1998*

### Tottenham Hotspur 1 Barnsley 1
### (FA Cup Fourth Round)

A dogged display earned Barnsley a replay. Sol Campbell scored for Tottenham after 30 minutes but Neil Redfearn equalised from the penalty spot after Ashley Ward had been fouled by Clive Wilson. Despite the win, Wilson admitted that he did not 'give a monkey's about the cup', preferring instead to focus on league survival.

Barnsley supporters were disappointed that Tottenham had no concessionary match tickets, so everyone, including children and pensioners, had to pay £18 for their seat. The car parks near White Hart Lane were charging £10 for a space.

———————

*Thursday 29 January 1998*

Danny Wilson had proved highly media-friendly. Despite the team's poor performances, he rarely turned down interviews and answered questions directly, even when the queries were banal and repetitive. Unlike most managers, he did not scurry on to the team coach in a sulk or, alternatively, play out his frustrations to a television camera. He was invariably composed, prepared to wisecrack, whatever the heartache.

Within a few short months he had, without any real effort or inclination, established himself as part of the fabric of the Premiership. Barnsley would lose, the nation would see the goals on television, and Wilson would appear on their screens. 'I thought we'd have to pass the calculator around at half-time to keep track of the score,' he would joke. Big smile, then a serious, I-mean-business-look. 'No, but in all honesty, we have to be willing to get a foot in, get among them ...'

Wilson was accepted into the nation's sporting psyche on a no-questions-asked basis. The media portrays football people as if their lives began when they signed for their first football club, so we are rarely privy to their formative years. Wilson was revered, branded as the sporting loser, a small man with a big heart, a man with whom it would be an honour to share a pint. Numerous articles ran in newspapers and magazines where he was taken purely on face value. The research was minimal, and no-one, it appeared, was prepared to countenance anything vaguely contrary to this newly-formed caricature.

I decided to write a piece about Wilson's background, chiefly about his days as a young footballer in the Wigan area. I had no ulterior motive, aside from unearthing some fresh, original copy. As the feature was to appear in the football section of a quality newspaper, I was plainly not searching for anything salacious or trite. This is not to say that I would not have used information unconnected to sport if it gave an insight into my subject; I considered this a basic constituent of journalism, so long as it was related fairly, in context, and without malice.

I sent a letter to the *Wigan Evening Post* and one of its reporters contacted me. The paper included a news item next to a small photo of Wilson. Unfortunately, despite my telling them so, it failed to mention that the resulting piece was to run in the football section of *The Times*. This meant my position as a 'freelance writer' appeared indeterminate, as if I might be interested in any personal tittle-tattle I could find – and sell, presumably. It read:

'Danny Wilson may not yet be one of Wigan's most famous sons but the town cannot boast too many Premiership managers.

'It is a long while since he left his Billinge home to become boss of Barnsley FC, but freelance writer Mark Hodkinson is hoping to speak to anyone who remembers Danny's years in the borough for a feature he intends writing.

'He said: "I would love to speak to any *Evening Post* readers who remember Danny, such as schoolmates, family and people he worked with – he worked at Ravenhead brickworks for nearly a year – so that I can get as full a picture of the man as possible."

'Anyone with any tales to tell can ring Mark on ...'

---

*Friday 30 January 1998*

Dark, cold night, the central heating up full. My 15-month-old son had learned another command, 'Knee, knee,' and between tea-time and bed-time, anyone sitting down would hear the plea, as he approached, book in hand.

We were halfway through his favourite story, 'We're Going On A Bear Hunt', a story using a rhythm of words to beat out the tale of a hapless family who go looking for a bear, only to find one and turn and flee. Finally, in the safety of their own bed, while the bear hammers at their door, they exclaim: 'We're not going on a bear hunt again.'

We were at the point where the family were stumble trip, stumble trip-tripping through a forest when the phone sounded. I had to disentangle myself and took a few seconds to take hold of the handset.

'Are you the person asking for information about Danny Wilson?' said the voice. He was talking quickly and loudly. At first, I imagined it was someone in a pub or club who had been shown a copy of the *Wigan Evening Post* and had decided to call straight away. The voice was familiar though.

After a few seconds, I recognised that it was Danny Wilson and asked him to confirm it was him. He did not answer, but continued to talk without stopping to breathe. 'What do you want to know all this stuff for? What right have you got to do things like this?'

He wanted to know who I was, so I explained I was the reporter who had spent almost three hours with him a few months earlier and that we had spoken regularly on the phone. He made no acknowledgment that he knew who I was, never used my first name.

'How do you think I'm supposed to feel?' he said, his voice now dry and shrill. 'My sister has just rung me and told me about someone trying to find out all about me.' I apologised and said I was sorry if it had upset him. 'You could have asked me first,' he said. I explained that he had previously failed to respond to some of my queries or contact me when a deadline had passed. 'I always get back to you,' he snapped. 'It might take some time. You wouldn't get an answer off Alex Ferguson the same day would you?'

His anger never subsided. In between the questions, he said continually, 'You're bang out of order here, bang out of order.' Towards the end of the conversation, he said more than once: 'You'd better watch yourself, you.' The phrase looks worse written down, but it was not delivered with any menace. It was anger thrown quickly and roughly into words. He put the phone down abruptly without any formal good-bye.

I was shocked, upset that he had disturbed the peace in my home. Naturally, for most of the evening my thoughts were malevolent. I had, at last, seen this man for what he really was. He was venerated as football's ultimate Everyman, but I knew him differently. I had seen the snapshot of Wilson spliced from the family photo album. He was aggressive, didactic, relentless.

CHAPTER SEVEN

A Bloody Sonnet

# LIFE AT THE TOP

## BARNSLEY HAPPY TO SHOP TILL THEY DROP
*(The Times, Saturday 31 January 1998)*

It is night-time at noon in Barnsley. Car headlights illuminate
rays of shooting rain, but otherwise there is nothing but damp,
dripping greyness. The middle-aged lady in the Reds
Superstore has picked up her first cold of 1998. Cough, cough,
she tidies some badges on the counter. Sniff, sniff, she runs her
hands across some shirts and flattens them straight. 'We won't
see many in here today, will we?' she sighs as she looks across
the rain-lashed car park. 'I feel a bit chilly as well.' Official
Barnsley paracetamols are not yet on sale, but if she needs to
keep warm she will find enough scarves to lag a house and a
choice of five different jackets.

On another day, when the rain moves on to Doncaster or
Sheffield, the store will be busy again. Very busy. Barnsley, the
corner-shop club, is no more. It has two superstores – one in the
town centre and the other at Oakwell – and while they are
nothing on the cavernous hypermarkets of Manchester United
and Chelsea, who they play today, their turnover during the
club's financial year is expected to reach £1 million.

The club's ascent through the leagues has been
complemented by an expansion of its commercial activities. Just
a few years ago, the whole of the club's merchandise was housed
in a glorified tea bar. 'They used to lift a flap up on match days
and you could only buy what you could see, which wasn't very
much,' said Clive Wood, superstore manager and a Barnsley
supporter for more than 40 years. 'Practically the only thing
supporters had in those days was a red-and-white scarf that
your mum or aunt had knitted you.'

Hundreds of items are now available carrying the official
'Toby Tyke' trademark, from bedspreads to bath foam, dog tags
to dungarees. 'I could see a rep every ten minutes if I wanted,'
said Wood. 'They are always trying to get us to stock new lines.'
One such item was a Barnsley toilet seat cover. 'It was fabulously
done,' he said. 'This couple came in with it. They were very
posh and had gone to a lot of trouble making a prototype, but

we couldn't have sold it. If it had been a Wolves toilet seat cover we might have taken them, though.' In explanation, there remains a simmering feud between Mark McGhee, the Wolverhampton Wanderers manager, and Barnsley after he made some sniffy comments about them last season.

Replica shirts are the main line of business and by the end of the season the club expects to have sold more than 10,000. They are priced at £36.99 for adults (which account for four-fifths of all shirt sales) and either £28.99 or £32.99 for children. Wood was surprised at the criteria for ordering new shirts. 'These lads would come in and I'd size them up straight away, guessing them to be a 38-inch chest, or whatever,' he said. 'They'd ask for extra large and I'd tell them it would bury them. They wouldn't have it, though. They didn't say anything at the time, but they were buying them to put over their coats or a few jumpers on cold days.'

It appears that a souvenir's practical use has little bearing on its popularity. When Wood was offered Barnsley seat cushions he imagined they would be in high demand, for Oakwell is noted for cold and damp. They have sold so poorly that he has started to offer them at a discount. He can sell Barnsley clotted cream caramels, red-and-white wigs, and knickers bearing the legend 'I scored at Barnsley', but seat cushions remain at the bottom of the sales league, so to speak.

There are several families who appear to be furnishing their entire homes in Barnsley mementoes and some have spent up to £400 in a single visit to the stores. Parents should be aware that Barnsley memorabilia can have a salutary effect on children. After buying her 11-year-old son a Barnsley bed cover, one mother returned and informed staff that he had taken to going to bed at 5 pm, such was his enthusiasm to wrap himself in the club colours.

While the club benefits from a certain level of fanaticism, its staff are often left bewildered by the sense of priority shown by some supporters. One morning, soon after opening, an excitable young man demanded to see a selection of their baby outfits. 'How old is he?' they asked. 'Let me see,' he said, opening out his fingers to count. 'Four hours.'

One of the cheapest items on sale, at just £1, are individual photographs of the first-team squad. Their sales are a good indicator of a player's repute. The pin-ups of the squad are strikers Andy Liddell and Ashley Ward, while Neil Redfearn and John Hendrie are popular with both male and female fans. And what of Georgi Hristov who thinks so much of the local ladies? 'Better not say,' Wood laughs. 'Nah, not too bad. I think we've sold one or two since he was supposed to have said all that Barnsley-birds-love-booze stuff.' More laughter ensues, all the way to the bank.

---

*Saturday 31 January 1998*

### Chelsea 2 Barnsley 0

Goals by Gianluca Vialli and Mark Hughes gave Chelsea a comfortable victory against a Barnsley side struggling to piece together attacking moves. 'Although we played well in the first half-hour, we did not really deserve anything from the game,' said Danny Wilson.

---

*Monday 2 February 1998*

Over the course of the weekend, my attitude towards Wilson had softened, and I began to rationalise his point of view. I imagined him receiving a call from his sister, perhaps in a slight state of panic, as he waited with the team in their London hotel on the eve of the match with Chelsea. Abruptly, his family life had collided with his professional existence and it left him feeling vulnerable and exposed.

There were other extenuating circumstances. Wilson is the king in his own kingdom. At Barnsley he is surrounded by people indebted to him, so he rarely hears a voice of dissent or complaint. Inevitably, in this situation, it would be difficult not to develop autocratic tendencies. Perhaps I also over-reacted to his aggressive manner. Away from the media pleasantries, football remains a coarse business, where the language is direct, the sentiment raw. He was sorting out the matter with the same 'industrial' approach he would use if one of his defenders had not marked a striker at a free-kick: 'I'll tell you this just once...'

On a professional level, I was concerned about possible repercussions. The season still had three months to run and my commission was to write a piece every week until the final game. If Wilson wished, he could ask staff at the club to remove their co-operation and ban me from Oakwell. *The Times*, incidentally, offered its absolute support; at the Sportsdesk they were clear that I had not done anything untoward, and promised to take matters to a higher level if required.

I phoned Wilson three times but the calls were not returned. I then sent a letter. It was more sycophantic than I would have wished, but the aim was to maintain my relationship with the club, as well as profile my own integrity:

Dear Danny,

I can fully understand your attitude on Friday. I would be disgruntled too if someone I didn't know was featured in a news story asking for information about me.

There were, however, mitigating circumstances and I hope you will hear me out. My intention was only ever to write a fairly whimsical piece about your early footballing days in Wigan. I was not digging for dirt. I work for *The Times* as a *football* reporter; the paper, and myself, have no interest in gossip, scandal, etc.

I merely wrote a letter to the Wigan paper. I expected it would make a small item on their letters page, but, apparently, they ran it as a fairly splashy news story. I can see that this would cause a degree of alarm [I did not see the article until a few weeks later. It was much smaller than I had been led to believe from Wilson's response].

Yes, I should, in hindsight, have let you know my intentions. In all honesty, though, I didn't think it would be a big deal. My intentions were honourable, it was not an attempt to be sneaky or malicious. I can see that, as it turned out, it looked that way, but I can assure you that it was simply a case of my enthusiasm getting the better of me.

For your information, the people who contacted me afterwards were ... Do you mind if I speak to them, or would you rather I ditch the whole idea? [I would have been reluctant to do this, but I wanted him to feel that I might acquiesce to his wishes].

Yours faithfully
Mark Hodkinson

--------

*Tuesday 3 February 1998*

Toby Tyke, the Barnsley club mascot, is probably the most cherished of its kind in English football. Children idolise him because he is cute and furry, while adults like his knowing, scampish sense of humour. A cartoon drawing of a tyke has been Barnsley's trademark for more than 25 years. When he left the page to become three-dimensional, it was not a tawdry attempt to follow fashion, or Americanise the club, it was – as far as these things can be – a natural development.

Toby justifies a good portion of the admission price at Oakwell. The team might be prone to erratic performances, but Toby is the model of consistency. Like the best performers, he plays the crowd to perfection. On a quiet, tense afternoon he might pad along the perimeter fence, shaking hands or sharing sweets, or he might prick the tension by charging down the centre of the pitch. He has a honed showbiz instinct, and Barnsley secure maximum returns from their genius in the dog-suit.

There were numerous potential subjects to profile at Oakwell, but Toby was essential. It would have seemed a simple procedure, but the club behaved strangely over the issue and although the piece – when it finally appeared – was written in a humorous vein, this silly, whimsical matter revealed the club at its worst.

Chris Patzelt had teased me playfully during an afternoon at the club. He made a big fuss of Toby's anonymity. 'Even we don't know who he is,' he fibbed. 'He lives in that kennel over there,' he said, pointing to a box by the car park gate.

He clearly relished Toby's notoriety: 'He's a naughty doggie sometimes.'

It took all of 10 minutes to discover the identity of 'Toby', though this was the easy part. I spoke to him on the phone and he appeared a likeable young man, though he was paranoid about my first receiving clearance from the club. 'Has Chris [Patzelt] said it's okay?' he asked. 'Does Michael [Spinks] know?' What had they done to Toby to make him so obedient, so fearful of his masters?

We arranged to meet at Oakwell, just three days after my argument with Danny Wilson. I decided that, while I was at the club, I would speak to Wilson and deal with the matter head-on. As it happens, he was not in; at least that is what I was told.

The receptionists, friendly as ever, informed me that they had not seen Toby, but that I should try the lottery office, situated 50 yards away. Here, a crabby man asked who I was and told me to wait. He returned after a few minutes and said gravely that I would need permission from Michael Spinks or Chris Patzelt before Toby would come out.

Dutifully, I walked back to the main reception and asked to see Spinks or Patzelt. 'Michael's not around and Chris is on the phone.' I asked them to put a note in front of Patzelt informing him that I needed a quick decision because Toby was on his lunch-break (he works as a barber in the town) and only had an hour to spare. 'Chris has someone with him and won't be able to come out all afternoon,' she said.

At this point, I was convinced that Wilson had told them not to deal with me, though no-one had the courage to tell me in person. The frustration was immense, the whole situation embarrassing. I had travelled over 50 miles to be spurned by a giant dog. It was so ridiculous, it was unbelievable. I returned to the lottery office prepared to tell the white lie that Toby had been given permission to speak to me, which he had tacitly since it was Patzelt's suggestion in the first place. 'Oh, he's just gone,' said the lottery man. Somehow, I expected as much.

---

*Wednesday 4 February 1998*

### Barnsley 3 Tottenham Hotspur 1
### (FA Cup Fourth Round Replay)

In a stirring cup-tie, Barnsley defeated Tottenham Hotspur 3-1 with goals from Ashley Ward, Neil Redfearn and Darren Barnard. David Ginola scored the Tottenham goal and his all-round display of industry matched with stately ball skills earned him the respect of the home crowd. Jürgen Klinsmann suffered a broken jaw after a collision with Arjan de Zeeuw. There were fears that he would be out for the rest of the season, but he was back in action within a few weeks.

Barnsley supporters were impressed that Ginola signed autographs and posed for photographs after the game. The victory set up a return to Old Trafford in the FA Cup Fifth Round, nearly four months after their 7-0 embarrassment in the league.

---

BARNSLEY EXTEND THEIR CUP VACATION
*(match report, The Times, Thursday 5 February 1998)*

Tradition and football are showing signs of parting company, but this was a magnificent swansong for the famous partnership. Four sublime goals, a sending-off, an avalanche of shots and shuddering tackles – this was a cup tie of historical proportions.

The only sour note was an injury to Jürgen Klinsmann, which left him unconscious and required prompt attention from medical staff, who thought he had swallowed his tongue.

Klinsmann had hurled himself recklessly towards the ball and landed awkwardly after colliding with de Zeeuw. After lengthy treatment, he was carried off. It was later confirmed that he had broken his jaw.

The FA Cup has given these teams a welcome break from their Premiership relegation battles and, last night, they played with the abandon of a game of beach soccer. It was end-to-end stuff, with little regard for minor irritants such as defending or playing to position. Tottenham had the better technique, Ginola especially, with his flicks and expansive passes, but Barnsley had the relentless death-or-glory drive which the Cup demands.

The supporters were also taken with the mood of traditionalism. A home-made replica of the FA Cup, coated in tin foil, was waved aloft by the Spurs contingent, while the ground fell into reverential silence as a Barnsley fan set a huge wooden rattle a-clicking. Barnsley had most of the early chances; Ward and Bullock missed narrowly, while a Redfearn punt careered inches past a post. Ginola played deep, keen to conduct Spurs' fluid formation, and was behind moves that saw Fox and Berti almost break the deadlock. Hendrie and Bullock danced blithely between the bulky frames of the visiting defenders and Baardsen had to remain vigilant to thwart the more linear attacks. Tottenham found themselves a player down in the 50th minute, when Clemence was sent off for diving in the penalty area as the Barnsley defence snapped at his heels. He had been booked in the 27th minute, for a foul on Eaden.

Before Tottenham had settled, Barnsley surged forward and Redfearn crossed for Ward to head the ball adroitly beyond Baardsen. The home side now held superiority and used the extra space to piece together their passing game. Tottenham's growing frustration was palpable as Ginola lifted a shot metres over the bar and Klinsmann scuffed a shot from deep inside the penalty area. The pulsating drama was distilled into a breathless minute of play. Tottenham tore forward and both Klinsmann and Ferdinand swiped at the ball as it rode inches from the goal-line. Morgan thumped it clear of the line and Barnsley pounced on the loose ball. Bullock, Barnsley's schoolboy-sized winger, collected and jigged towards goal, evading tackles with a deft swivel of the hips. His shot was saved but Redfearn, made of beefier stock, crashed the ball defiantly into the net.

Ward turned home a Bullock cross but was ruled offside as Barnsley colonised the Tottenham half. Barnard shot from distance and, though Baardsen appeared unperturbed, it rattled the goal-post. Vega mounted a solo raid, but was interrupted, illegally, by Morgan. Ginola flicked the hair from his eyes and gave a similar subtle touch to the ball, as he lifted the free kick beyond Watson to reduce the deficit. Barnsley, quite rightly, had the final say in the final minute, when Redfearn fed Barnard, who scooped the ball above and beyond Baardsen. The Tottenham supporters began to leave in droves. The game was lost and the sight of Vega, a makeshift striker, lumbering aimlessly towards goal merely confirmed that all their options had been exhausted. A long battle to avoid relegation is all that remains for Tottenham to contemplate this season.

Barnsley remain unbeaten in their past eight home matches and the locals will swear that this form, now embracing a Cup run, amounts to a renaissance of sorts. Manchester United await in the fifth round.

---

*Thursday 5 February 1998*

I received a two-line note from Danny Wilson reading:

> In reply to your letter of Monday February 2nd 1998. I have no power to stop you doing anything you wish if you feel it will make good reading, it is entirely your decision.

> Yours sincerely
> Danny Wilson

By this point, I was demoralised by Barnsley. I had written a series of complimentary pieces about the club, with precious little assistance from them – and hindrance on occasions – yet, because of one assumed transgression, my letter of apology warranted a mere two-line response; two lines that seemed to set me some kind of moral test.

The Toby Tyke article had been completed and was waiting to run. Otherwise, I resolved to spend the next few weeks working on pieces that did not necessitate a visit to Oakwell. I did not want to go near the place.

*Friday 6 February 1998*

Plaques were unveiled at Oakwell and Darfield Foulstone School, Barnsley, in memory of Tommy Taylor and Mark Jones, two Barnsley-born footballers who died in the Munich air disaster 40 years before, while members of the famous Manchester United team dubbed the Busby Babes. Taylor made 44 league appearances for his home-town club before joining United for a record fee of £29,999. Jones had been understudy to Allenby Chilton but, at 24, had established himself as an influential member of the United team. Jones's older brother, Amos, wrote a poem about his brother, which included the lines: 'He always was the gentleman in action and in thought, / He always thought of others, that's what his parents taught.'

———

KES, SWEET BIRD OF BARNSLEY YOUTH
*(The Times, Saturday 7 February 1998)*

The wind and the mud; the PE teacher with thighs like beer barrels and a voice like bloody hell; the scrawny, pencil-thin kids using their shirt cuffs as handkerchiefs; goose pimples and chattering teeth; we've all been there. It was August in Barnsley and the sun should have been warming their backs, but a chill wind chuckled vindictively across the playing fields of St

Helen's Secondary Modern School. The film crew were constantly offering hot drinks to their extras of local schoolchildren, but in their hearts they knew that every shiver, grimace and bored expression were the very currency of their film.

The schoolboy footballers in Kes were playing for England, the picture of England drawn by Barry Hines in his book *A Kestrel for a Knave*, on which the film was based. Mr Sugden, the PE teacher played unforgettably by the late Brian Glover, decreed that it was Manchester United versus Spurs in a fifth-round Cup tie, but it was really a far more important encounter. It was the disillusioned versus the disadvantaged, the bully versus the bullied. What chance had they when Sugden was both Bobby Charlton ('I'm scheming this morning, all over the field') and the referee?

In the course of the most infamous games lesson in British history, Hines used football as the consummate metaphor of life. Billy Casper, the book's protagonist, is a dreamy, downtrodden waif in borrowed shorts. He is made the scapegoat when 'Manchester United' lose 4-3. Afterwards, he is imprisoned in the showers and Sugden slyly moves the temperature gauge to its lowest setting. 'He'll get pneumonia,' plead Casper's classmates. 'I don't care what he gets,' Sugden snaps. Suddenly, Casper appears at the top of the partition wall. He has climbed free and is greeted by uproarious laughter; an away win for the disadvantaged.

Football has seldom transferred well onto the page or screen. Hines is one of a handful of writers with an innate ability to present sport without the schmaltz. To him, football is the reflection of the lives from which it offers a fleeting respite. It is a slog, against cheats and bullies, kickers and cloggers, and the last man standing tall in the mud can claim a victory of sorts.

Hines was introduced to the game by his grandfather, John Hines, a gifted local footballer. While he was growing up in the mining village of Hoyland Common, Barnsley, and earning praise for his own footballing ability, Hines would be told constantly: 'Tha'll never be as good as tha grandfather.' He applied himself better than his grandfather, who was, according to Hines, 'a bit of a wide boy', and played for the junior teams of both Barnsley and Wolverhampton Wanderers, before being selected to play for England grammar schools against Scotland in 1957.

While studying physical education at Loughborough Training College, Hines wrote the draft of his first novel, *The Blinder*. Brian Glanville had earlier published *The Rise of Gerry Logan*, widely regarded as the first football novel. Before these, there had been two types of football books – works of fiction that were fanciful and superficial and others on a theme of 'My Life in Football', whereby old pros would bolster their pension-plan by putting their names to a bloodless autobiography.

*The Blinder*, published in 1966 when Hines was 27, takes the reader inside the dressing-room, where the clank-clanking of studs resonates and the language is as strong as the tackles out on the pitch. Word filtered through to Hines several years ago that a former professional had read the book and commented: 'Whoever wrote that book knows about football.' It is a compliment he holds dear. 'I see the book now as crude, but it has a lot of vitality. When you are young and full of it, that is the type of book you write,' he said.

He became absorbed into the culture of football by both playing the game and watching Barnsley. 'There used to be four of us who went to Oakwell. We'd get there about an hour and a half before the kick-off. As soon as they opened the turnstiles we would rush down the terraces to stand directly behind the goal. I don't know why we always ran, because we'd be the only ones in there anyway at that time.'

During one match he noticed a football stud near the perimeter fence, priceless treasure to a smitten youngster. He hurried over and scooped it up. 'I got home and my dad said 'What have you got that for?' I said it might have belonged to a Barnsley player, maybe Skinner Normanton or Jimmy Baxter, but he just didn't understand. I remember being upset by his response.'

Hines writes his books and television dramas in a tiny office on the campus of Sheffield Hallam University, where he is an honorary Fellow. A line of postcards, most of them miniatures of famous paintings, adorn a shelf; otherwise it is spartan, save for a kettle designed to hold enough water to fill just one cup. He does not have a word processor and writes his material in pen before passing it on to be typed. He volunteers that he does not drive, nor own a video recorder. 'It's madness, I know. We've got a telly, but we've had that for about 20 years and it's only a small one,' he said.

He is lithe and his movements quick and precise. When the words run out he springs from his chair. 'And he would turn his back like this ...' he said. For a moment or so, he is Tony Currie, and then Denis Law, dancing beyond imaginary defenders in this small, dark room. He then sits back down and reflects for a few seconds, aware once more of his surroundings. His personality is very much like his writing – thoughtful but matter-of-fact, unadorned, effervescent and, as in his books, he can sometimes drift away, suspended in his own thoughts.

A smile is imprinted across his face when he recalls Barnsley's promotion to the Premiership. In his work, he invokes the occasional dash of other-worldly magic as a counter point to the relentless itchy realism. Barnsley in the top division still holds this sense of magic for Hines, nearly ten months after promotion was secured. 'It is absolutely wondrous,' he said. 'I never imagined them in the top division. I can remember when they were in the old fourth.'

He is not a frequent visitor to Oakwell these days and – better whisper this in Barnsley – often lends his support to Sheffield United. In mitigation, he proffers that he now lives in Sheffield and has a son who is a Blades fanatic. 'I saw Barnsley at Bramall Lane a few years ago and it was a strange experience. They were wearing blue and it didn't seem too bad, but when I see Barnsley in red I feel all the old pride coming back. It's like first love, isn't it?' While Barnsley found themselves adopted by a clutch of celebrities at the end of last season, Hines preferred to court the shadows. 'I would have felt like a carpet-bagger after all this time,' he said. For him, football is too important, too enmeshed in people's lives for half-measures. While his club loyalties are divided, the football man within him remains steadfastly authentic.

———————

*Saturday 7 February 1998*

**Barnsley 2 Everton 2**

Barnsley were the better side, but had to settle for a point against an uninspiring Everton. Jan-Aage Fjortoft and Darren Barnard scored, while the visitors' goals came from Duncan Ferguson and Tony Grant. 'It shows how far we have progressed that we are disappointed with a draw against a team of Everton's standards,' said Wilson. He was not to know that Everton would have one of their worst-ever seasons, avoiding relegation by goal difference.

———————

*Sunday 15 February 1998*

**Manchester United 1 Barnsley 1
(FA Cup Fifth Round)**

More than 100 coaches ferried 8,500 Barnsley supporters to Old Trafford where they witnessed a memorable game. John Hendrie, recalled to the team because Jan-Aage Fjortoft was cup-tied, gave Barnsley the lead after an amazing blunder by Peter Schmeichel. The goalkeeper miss-hit a clearance and Hendrie raced in to score. 'I just thought I'd better get my little legs going like the clappers but it felt like it was happening in slow motion – like in *Chariots Of Fire*,' said Hendrie.

Teddy Sheringham equalised for United but in the dying minutes substitute Andy Liddell looked set to score a winner when he was brought down by Gary Neville. Mike Riley, the referee, turned down penalty appeals. Alex Ferguson admitted afterwards: 'It was a definite penalty.'

De Zeeuw Eager To Spring To Barnsley's Defence
*(The Times, Saturday 21 February 1998)*

The rain lashed down, the moors conspired with the darkness to shut out the skyline and Arjan de Zeeuw, quite understandably, pondered suddenly: 'Where am I going?' Barnsley in November, especially at nightfall, can be a daunting experience, even for brave souls wandering across the border from distant climes such as Wakefield or Doncaster. The welcome they receive will be guarded and a bit reluctant, but at least they will understand it.

'Eh up, are yer reet?' was the reception awaiting de Zeeuw, Barnsley's Dutch centre back, on one of his first visits to the town. He repeats the phrase, in perfect English of course, and it takes on an hilarious touch. His English is exemplary and his Yorkshire is coming along grand, too, though he has recently started to pick up the meaningless phrases that litter football's vocabulary. 'In all fairness ...' he begins. Esther, his wife, corrects him immediately. 'Why do you keep saying that?' His smile turns upside down. 'I don't know, do I say it a lot?' He laughs at himself and, thereafter, each time the phrase escapes, he chides himself, sometimes thumping his fist onto his thigh in exasperation.

'Barnsley? I've never heard of it!' was his response when first told by his agent that they had been monitoring his progress. He had spent three seasons with Telstar in the Dutch First Division, after delaying his entry into the professional game to complete a degree in the science of movement at the University of Amsterdam. 'My agent told me about the town, about the mining history and the unemployment,' he said. 'He said it had been through a lot but that the football club was working its way up and doing quite well.' After that disconcerting first night in Barnsley in 1995, de Zeeuw woke up to find the sun shining on the town. 'Everything looks better in the sunshine, doesn't it?' he said. 'They showed me around the place and were very honest with me. It was better that way, because I would have only found out later if it had been a dump. Danny Wilson was very charismatic and told me how he wanted the team to play.'

De Zeeuw was born in Castricum, a small village on the coast of Holland, where weekends would involve trips to the beach or walks through the woods. The pace of life was languid and the cultural contrast to Barnsley distinct. De Zeeuw, like many of his countrymen, is the epitome of tolerance and open-mindedness. He has a problem with the British attachment to flowery wallpaper and carpets in bathrooms, but he finds our other idiosyncrasies – most of them, anyway – a joy.

'Mushy peas? How do you eat mushy peas? Everyone had told me about fish and chips and I got some with mushy peas on top. Awful. Sometimes we used to stop the coach on the way back from games and have fish and chips. I couldn't believe it. I used to give mine away, I couldn't eat it.' In his home, a new but unpretentious house on the fringes of Barnsley, he prefers to serve Dutch biscuits. 'He only wants you to have one so he can have another one too,' said Esther. They are large and sticky, probably just a calorie or two short of a plate of Barnsley's best chips. 'And you want coffee too?' asks de Zeeuw. He detects a slight hesitation. 'Dutch coffee, stronger than yours,' he volunteers. The deal is done.

De Zeeuw was the first of a crop of foreign players to join Barnsley and he has adapted effortlessly, both to the English game and the way of life. 'The pace of the football is so much quicker over here,' he said. 'English centre forwards will try and tackle you; that would rarely happen in Holland. Over there you could more or less walk with the ball to the halfway line.'

His popularity within the club is a testament to a personality that is direct but guileless, intelligent but unadorned. There is always a smile on his lips and the playful shrug of the shoulder. Everything is 'no problem'. Sure, we can take photographs of him in his living room. Sure, we can rearrange the furniture to get a better shot. Sure, we can put our coffee cups on the polished wood floor. 'I think the English are too formal,' he said. 'We will do what we fancy. We might call on a friend and stay there for half an hour or for eight hours, it depends on how we feel.'

De Zeeuw is under intensive treatment for a groin strain he suffered during Barnsley's drawn FA Cup fifth-round tie with Manchester United on Sunday. 'It happened on the 23rd minute and 10 seconds,' he said, with the mournful accuracy of a man who has replayed the match video once too often. 'I went up for a header and the other player landed right on a place where I had already been sore.' He is optimistic that he will recover for the replay at Oakwell on Wednesday. Earlier this week, while on the treatment table, he told Michael Tarmey, the club physiotherapist, that he had dreamt of Barnsley reaching Wembley. 'I couldn't believe it,' said de Zeeuw. 'He told me that he had also had the dream.'

De Zeeuw's father, Cees, was a United supporter until his son signed for Barnsley. His favourite player was Nobby Stiles. 'He liked him because he was an aggressive little man who could also play good football,' said de Zeeuw. He was unaware that Dennis Bergkamp had been named after another Manchester United player of the same era, Denis Law. 'Oh no,' he said eventually. 'I might have been called Nobby.' Nobby de Zeeuw, in all fairness, would take some living down, especially in Barnsley.

---

*Saturday 21 February 1998*

### Coventry City 1 Barnsley 0

The match was dire and uneventful until the final minutes when the referee, Alan Wilkie, awarded Coventry City a penalty for a 'push' on Dion Dublin. Peter Markstedt, the Barnsley player nearest Dublin, claimed he had made no contact and television replays showed that his arms had remained by his side as Dublin fell dramatically to the pitch. Dublin himself scored the penalty. Scott Jones, a 22-year-old who had almost left the club to join Mansfield Town, made his Premiership début in the Barnsley defence.

'It was not a penalty,' said Danny Wilson. 'I think I'm going to have to change my attitude to referees. I'm going to start ranting and raving and slagging them off. Perhaps then we would start getting decisions to go our way.' He did not carry out his threat, and maintained the poise that won him so many admirers during the season.

---

*Wednesday 25 February 1998*

### Barnsley 3 Manchester United 2
### (FA Cup Fifth Round Replay)

An exhilarating cup tie finished 3-2 after Barnsley had led 2-0 at half-time with goals from John Hendrie and Scott Jones. Teddy Sheringham pulled one back before Jones headed his second of the game. Andy Cole scored nine minutes before the end but Barnsley held on for a famous victory, despite six minutes of injury time. 'Never in a million years did I dream anything like this might happen. Not so long ago, I thought I was on my way,' said Scott Jones. 'The win is one of the best Barnsley Football Club has ever had,' added Wilson.

The match was televised live by Sky and did much to win Barnsley support throughout the country. United were not magnanimous in defeat; five of their players were booked and they showed a great deal of ill-temper and frustration as they failed to break down Barnsley's rearguard. Before the game, their players had refused to leave the team coach, complaining that the visitors' dressing room was too small. Eventually, a police officer boarded and told them they would have to get off, or risk having it towed away.

It was undoubtedly the highlight of Barnsley's season. The win at Anfield was remarkable, but the cup victory had been on home soil, witnessed at close quarters by thousands of Barnsley fans, and shared by millions watching on television. Many wanted to freeze the moment, and supporter Peter Doherty gave it a qualified immortality when he had the scoreline included in new double glazing installed at his home in Commonwealth View, Bolton. 'I want to be constantly reminded of what they have achieved this season,' he said.

The official Barnsley club poet, Ian McMillan, was approached after the game by an enthusiastic fan and told: 'Tha'll not write a poem abaht that, tha'll write a bloody sonnet!'

---

## OLD MOORE'S ALMANACK GETS A NEW CHAPTER
*(The Times, Saturday 28 February 1998)*

The final whistle sounded and they danced in glee, punched the air, and sang to the night sky. Victory against Manchester United, especially in the FA Cup, is a special event and the whole of Barnsley has claimed the glory as its own. Within the protocol of football support, however, there is a hierarchy of allegiance and the club's success, while shared by many, belongs to some more than others.

Amid the celebrations on Wednesday night, a quiet reflective figure in Row H, seat 52, of Oakwell's West Stand afforded himself a smile. Afterwards, he lingered in the vice-president's lounge, savouring the moment. It was, after all, the eve of his 93rd birthday and the euphoria of a win against United is not to be drunk quickly, like a glass of cheap wine. 'It was a terrific match,' said Frank Moore. 'It was all about team spirit and I think every tribute should be made to our manager.' Barnsley have many loyal supporters but it is unlikely that any can match the devotion of Frank. He first attended Oakwell in 1913. Since then, apart from periods away at boarding school, he has missed no more than six home matches in 85 years, and for much of the time he has lived more than 40 miles from the ground. 'He will get out of bed with flu to go to Barnsley,' said his wife, Mary. 'He has missed weddings, christenings, all kinds of things down the years. I've never got angry about it. I've always been tolerant of Frank's football. I understand how much it means to him.'

The couple married on 1 September 1945, during a time when Football League matches had been suspended because of the Second World War. Barnsley were playing in the impromptu North League and East Midlands League, and, as Mary remembers, Frank was 'horrified' that he would have to miss a Barnsley match. They live in a bungalow in Buxton, Derbyshire. They moved there when he became a safety officer at ICI, which has a plant in the town. Frank is a smart man, a tie is worn at all times and a spotted handkerchief pokes out neatly from the breast pocket of his jacket. He has a stick by his chair to help him walk and his hearing fails him occasionally. Mary, though, listens on his behalf, and will answer, as well, if he ponders for too long.

Although he has few souvenirs, aside from the odd press cutting in an envelope marked 'Oakwell Memories', Frank can recall the past in piquant detail and provides a fascinating snapshot of football's past. During his first season as a supporter, Barnsley's league rivals were teams such as Glossop and Leeds City. Fans would take pigeons to games and release them at regular intervals with score updates fastened to their legs. Frank was also used as a messenger when, aged 14, he was told to relay the news that Barnsley had beaten West Bromwich Albion in the first round of the FA Cup. A mighty cheer rang out in the Strafford Arms Hotel in Stainborough when he arrived and, after he had drawn breath, he added: ' ... and Brough Fletcher scored the goal'.

Players would leave the Oakwell pitch after games via a roped-off path through the crowd and make their way to the dressing-room past piles of coke that was used to heat the laundry room. There were two notices in the home dressing-room. One appealed for clean living and fitness, while the other read: 'Please don't ask for complimentary tickets. If your friends will not pay to see you play, how can you expect strangers to?'

The legacy of supporting Barnsley was handed down to Frank by his father, Copley, a colliery secretary and commercial manager, who was a director and later president of the club for nearly 50 years. During one of the club's financial crises, Copley mortgaged the family home so that the players would receive their wages. Frank has seen thousands of players in the red of Barnsley and they come alive once more as he describes them in appropriate terms. Arthur Kaye (1950-58) was a 'little wasp at outside right'; Gordon Pallister (1938-51) 'could have had the telegraphic address, "stylish Barnsley"'; Danny McGarry (1938-39) was 'a peach of a left winger'. Danny Blanchflower arrived at Oakwell from Glentoran, the Northern Ireland club, in 1948 and became a crowd favourite immediately. 'We were playing Chesterfield one time and they had a brute playing centre half,' said Frank. 'Blanchflower had been fouled about five times and kept bouncing off him. I was sat in the directors' box and I said to one of our directors: 'He's a nasty big rough devil, isn't he?' He said: "Yes, I wish we had him!"'

With Mary, Frank attended many away matches, driving to the South of England when road journeys were fraught and could take a whole weekend. 'We stopped for a cup of tea once in a lay-by on the way to Bristol. The team coach came past and when they saw the Barnsley registration number on my car, all the players began to wave,' he said. Barnsley is now a buoyant, successful club, but Moore can recall vividly the times of financial crisis when survival meetings were held throughout the town and he regularly manned stalls at jumble sales. There were also the bleak days in the 1970s when Barnsley spent seven seasons in the Fourth Division, with attendances sometimes below 2,000. 'When we got promotion last year it was a reward for the disappointments we have had over many years,' said Frank. 'I didn't shed a tear of joy when we beat Bradford to go up, but I sat back and really enjoyed it once we went two goals in front and the anxiety had lifted.'

He still attends every home game, and although he drives, he prefers not to deal with the heavy traffic around Oakwell on match days. His car is driven by Roy Pickles, another Barnsley fan living in Buxton, a 'young chap' in his fifties. Moore will watch the FA Cup quarter-final at Newcastle United on television with a glass of sherry at hand. After that, it will be business as usual and a return to the fortnightly pilgrimage to Oakwell. 'He has gone there in two feet of snow and when it's been thick with fog. He's not going to change now, is he?' said Mary. She already knows the answer.

---

Journalism grants several privileges, but few as refreshing as spending time with people rich in personality and humility like Frank Moore. After years of relative anonymity, where his support for Barnsley had been noted by just a few, he suddenly found himself celebrated as the club's most stately supporter. After the article appeared, he was tracked down by other journalists and the story of his unflinching loyalty was retold in many publications. He was also featured on *Match Of The Day*, taking his seat before a Barnsley match.

He wrote me a note afterwards, worried because the photograph of his father had not been returned. His good humour, like his love of Barnsley, was clearly still intact: 'I am getting rather concerned that our Nottingham good-looker "film-star type" photographer hasn't returned my father's photo which is so precious to me. You kindly said you'd give him a nudge; I'd be so grateful if you could; but do apologise for troubling you about this.'

During one of the final home games of the season, the call rang out in the press room at Oakwell for 'the man from *The Times*'. Reporters dread this, for it is invariably a complaint. At the door, leaning on his walking stick, was Frank: 'I'd like to thank you so much,' he said. 'Since that article, I've become a proper celebrity, I can tell you.'

---

*Saturday 28 February 1998*

**Barnsley 2 Wimbledon 1**

Two goals from Jan-Aage Fjortoft lifted Barnsley from the bottom of the table, a place where they would never again return. Jason Euell pulled one back 19 minutes before the end to ensure another tense finish.

Vinnie Jones made himself unpopular when he walked through a throng of young Barnsley supporters after the match and promised he would return to sign autographs. Once on the team bus, he refused to budge, even when one of their fathers clambered on board to ask him to fulfil the promise.

# CHAPTER EIGHT

## A Nation of One

## TOBY TYKE AND THE MASK OF MYSTERY
*(The Times, Saturday 7 March 1998)*

As assignments go, it should be easy enough. It's not like asking Chris Sutton to autograph an England shirt or Gordon Strachan to list his favourite referees.* 'Toby Tyke, please,' is the request. 'Hmmm, now you're asking,' is the response.

Toby is the official mascot of Barnsley FC and, while the club is a new addition to the Premiership, Toby has been in the elite since he first strutted (walking is for cissies) on to the Oakwell pitch four years ago. Toby, see, is not one of those lightweight, fairy-cake mascots that shuffle apologetically along the perimeter fence. He is the authentic Yorkshire tyke – irreverent, energetic, drunk on life. If he's not barking in your face, he's barking at the moon. His antics have made the front page of the *Daily Sport* and the club has twice issued missives calling for a tad more decorum. All the same, he is much loved at Oakwell; in fact, his colour photograph is in more demand at the Reds Superstore than most of the players'.

If a superstar is measured by his degree of availability, Toby is Barnsley's answer to Prince or Bruce Springsteen. 'You'll have to put the request to Michael,' said the receptionist. 'Michael' is Michael Spinks, the club's general manager/secretary no less, and self-appointed dog-handler. Calls to him are not returned and a trip to Oakwell proves fruitless despite Toby's presence at the ground. 'He won't see you until Michael says it's OK.' Spinks is on the phone and then has a meeting. It is all academic anyway, Toby has scarpered.

Finally, on the blind side of Spinks, Toby is tracked down – only by phone, mind. 'You won't put in my real name will you?'

---

* Chris Sutton, the Blackburn Rovers striker, had turned down the opportunity to play for the England B team in their friendly match with Chile. He finished the season as the Premiership's top scorer, but his attitude meant he was not considered by Glenn Hoddle for the World Cup squad in the summer.

On *Match of the Day* Gordon Strachan, the Coventry City manager, had fumed about Steve Lodge, the Barnsley-born referee. He dubbed him a 'joke and a disgrace' for sending off the Coventry player, Paul Williams, after an alleged trip on Dennis Bergkamp.

he asked nervously. Instinctively, I ask him to wait while I draw the blinds and check the tip of my umbrella for unusual substances. Anonymity is promised and The Artist Actually Known As Toby (TAAKAT) turns out to be a charming, guileless 19 year-old who, when not dressed as a dog, albeit one who stands on two legs and wears a football kit, works as a barber in Barnsley.

'The mascot job is great for me,' he explained. 'I like messing about and acting the prat. When I go out with my mates on a Friday night there's always someone losing an eyebrow or something.' His notoriety owes much to a toilet roll, a toilet gesture and a set of Manchester City supporters who have had their noses rubbed in it once too often for their liking. 'They said I dropped my trousers but I didn't,' he pleaded. 'I just wiped my backside, that's all, and the City fans got a right monk on.' A 'monk', incidentally, is Barnsleyspeak for a bad mood, and not someone of a religious persuasion and a Howard Kendall haircut.

In the midst of the tabloid furore, Toby almost resigned, in appropriately melodramatic fashion. 'They were writing all this stuff and I thought "Bugger it." I was going to take my head off in the middle of the pitch.' By 'my head' he means Toby's head, of course; the groundsman might have complained otherwise. His other misdemeanour saw him knock off a policeman's helmet during Barnsley's on-pitch promotion party last season. 'He wrote a letter to the paper and said I'd set a bad example and all the kids would start doing the same thing now,' he said. Horror videos, violent computer games, Toby Tyke, their influence should be monitored.

Most of the time, Toby is a loveable rascal and his adoration is such that he is invited to birthday parties around the town. 'I've seen other mascots and they're not a patch on me. They don't do half the stuff I do,' he said. Lofty the Lion, Bolton Wanderers' furry talisman, is similarly triumphal, I proffer. Toby has more portentous news on the Lofty front. 'I heard he got pork pies thrown at him at a recent match. You've got to watch that, it's important to know just how to treat the away fans.'

One imagines a special relationship between a man and his mascot suit. When the performance is over and the suit is propped up lifeless and still, is there a moment of quiet reflection? 'You're too knackered to feel owt. It's hard work in that suit, you sweat a right lot.' The suit is due for replacement soon and the new one will be a different hue of brown. The children who watch his every swagger will be informed that Toby has had a bath and is showing his true colours.

The Artist Actually Known As Toby does not receive payment for his services, but has a seat reserved in an executive box. The offer of wages would be declined anyway: he's delighted to walk the hallowed turf and to support the club in such a unique way. He has two scrapbooks filled with cuttings about Toby Tyke and his bedroom wall is a shrine to this man-sized dog. A photograph, perhaps of TAAKAT in the half-light next to his suit, would at least show there is someone in there. The request is turned down. A local hack offers empathy. 'I found myself saying to someone at the club, "Come on, you know as well as I do that there is a bloke in there."' There is indeed a bloke in there, but such is the enigma surrounding Toby Tyke, he may soon prefer to linger outside the butchers rather than the barbers. The staff at Barnsley should be afraid, very afraid, of meddling with half-man, half-dog legends.

---

The club's determination to keep Toby's identity confidential is difficult to fathom. They went to extraordinary lengths, and had done so before with other journalists. Toby, in his own right, is marvellous PR for the club, but the rigmarole about his anonymity works to negate much of this.

An insider (another unwilling to step out of the shadows!) said the bizarre policy stemmed from Michael Spinks. He is an obsessive, dedicated wholly to Barnsley FC. Staff cannot remember when he last took a holiday, or had just a day away from his desk at Oakwell. Some feel he is occasionally over-protective and that his zeal can manifest itself as unnecessary secrecy.

During my conversation with 'Toby', it was apparent that he is, in Barnsley parlance, a 'bit of a lad'. He is amiable, funny (without trying to be), down-to-earth, easy-going, but probably without the drive or inclination to cast off his suit and adapt his theatrical bent to any other stage but Oakwell. My guess is that the club has the misguided belief that if he was allowed to reveal his real personality, he would not reflect well, but he is the authentic tyke with or without suit. He is happy to remain anonymous, afraid not to in fact, because he was born to the job, and his life would be a lot less pleasurable if he parted company with his furry suit.

---

*Sunday March 8 1998*

### Newcastle United 3 Barnsley 1
### (FA Cup Quarter-Final)

Temuri Ketsbaia and Gary Speed gave Newcastle an early lead but Andy Liddell pulled one back after half-time. Barnsley looked set for an equaliser before Adie Moses was sent off for the first time in his career after a mistimed tackle on Alan Shearer. Seconds before the final whistle, David Batty clinched the tie for Newcastle.

Newcastle showed little courtesy to Barnsley, refusing permission for Toby Tyke to undertake his usual routine and banning the official Barnsley backing group, the Ora Band, for 'safety reasons'. Barnsley supporters also found themselves dispersed in three separate sections around the ground.

The behaviour of Alan Shearer caused much comment afterwards. Three players were booked for challenges on him and many Barnsley supporters felt he had made the incidents appear far worse than they really were. John Dennis suggested to newsmen that Shearer received the same protection as an endangered species.

Later in the season, Shearer looked set to be called before the FA after he appeared to kick Neil Lennon, the Leicester City captain, in the face. No action was taken though, presumably because it would have had an unsettling influence on the England captain on the eve of a World Cup campaign. All the same, there was a growing suspicion among Barnsley fans that players with big-name clubs were being granted special privileges by referees.

After the match, police were called to two pubs in Darlington where Barnsley supporters had stopped off on the return journey. Trouble flared and £2000 of damage was caused to Yates's Wine Lodge where a doorman suffered a broken arm. Six weeks later police arrested a group of Barnsley supporters in dawn raids and they were charged with public order offences.

---

*Wednesday 11 March 1998*

### Aston Villa 0 Barnsley 1

A gritty defensive display earned Barnsley a valuable victory with a goal by Ashley Ward. Aston Villa dominated throughout, with 16 shots on goal, compared to Barnsley's three.

After the game, Ward was linked with Celtic who were reportedly about to table a £3 million offer. 'It would not surprise me that other clubs are interested in him because he has been outstanding this season, but he is going nowhere,' snapped John Dennis.

---

LONELY HEARTS AND THE GAME OF TWO HALVES
*(The Times, Saturday 14 March 1998)*

Imagine the advert. It would hardly sparkle in the lonely hearts column: 'Young man, fit and healthy, seeks attractive partner. Must be willing to sacrifice family, friends, career and be prepared to move around the country – possibly abroad – at a moment's notice. The world must revolve around me, and my fabulous career, at all times.'

The truth has many guises, of course, and the same person might decide upon a rewrite, and sit back while a fleet of Post Office vans arrive at the front door. The new version, with added efficacy, reads: 'Professional footballer, wealthy, famous, seeks wife.' Form an orderly queue, ladies.

There are approximately 2,500 professional footballers in England. We know a great deal about just a few of them. We know them the way we know stars of pop, film or television. They are sleek people with sleek cars, big on property and investments, big on themselves. Their mobiles ring constantly and, hey, these guys are popular, on the move, busy, busy; immaculate house, beautiful wife. If this stereotype fits, say, at most, 150 footballers, it amounts to only a small percentage of the total. The rest move among us largely unnoticed, save for the strange hours that they keep and their rather limited wardrobe of tracksuits and more tracksuits. These footballers share similar wages to supporters, live in similar houses and their lives are flushed with glamour only when the clock strikes three on Saturday.

John Hendrie, the Barnsley striker, is somewhere between the two versions of the modern footballer. He has played for seven clubs in a career embracing more than 600 appearances in all four divisions. He is recognised, but not famous; comfortable, but not wealthy. If his is the typical footballer's story, his wife, Linda, has lived the life typical of a footballer's partner. 'It's a good life but you have got to put up with a lot. I am a patient and placid person which has helped. You've not got to moan, you just get on with it and have to be prepared to take a back seat,' she said.

The couple met in 1982 when Hendrie was a young professional at Coventry City. Linda Burgess worked as a hairdresser in the town and remembers that he had the 'nicest blue eyes' she had ever seen. 'He was so shy, he wouldn't even look in the mirror while I was cutting his hair. I had to keep pulling his head up because he was staring down all the time,' she said.

Hendrie was given a free transfer to Bradford City and, though it ensured him a first-team place, it was far from glamorous. 'He was living in a horrible rented house with two other young players,' said Linda. 'I used to spend all weekend cleaning it. John actually caught scabies from the settee and there was damp everywhere. I can smell the place even now.' Until she met Hendrie, Linda had never attended a football match. Her first introduction to football's peculiar inner world of tea urns and triangular sandwiches, team sheets and commissionaires, was at a Bradford City home match against Doncaster Rovers. 'John got elbowed in the face. I remember being really upset and angry about it. I was a bit nervous. It's always like that when John goes to a new club, but once they get to know you, most people are chatty and OK.'

They married in June 1985 and moved into a terraced house in Leeds. His career took an upswing three years later when he joined Newcastle United. While he was being exalted, Linda recalls it as a time of abject misery. 'We moved into this detached bungalow in Darras Hall, the snobbiest part of Newcastle. I had two babies, one literally under each arm, and didn't know a soul. The washing was piling up, I didn't know where the nearest shop was. I just hated it and felt like crying,' she said.

The mood of despondency was compounded by concern over their newly-born son, Joe, whom doctors felt might have had a blockage in his brain. Joe's condition was transient and Linda eventually settled in Newcastle, though it was hardly worth the effort. After just one season, Hendrie arrived back in West Yorkshire when he joined Leeds United. Linda was pleased about a return to the region, but Hendrie phoned home within a few weeks of arriving there. 'Wilko [Howard Wilkinson, then the Leeds manager] is not for me,' he told her. This was football's vernacular but she understood all too well; they would soon be on the move again.

'I was at home one day and I took a call from Colin Todd,' said Linda. 'I did not know who he was but I had a feeling he was a manager from somewhere. It was on my mind all day. I knew John was unhappy at Leeds but I didn't want to move house again. Everything was still in boxes from the last move. Joe had lived in five different houses and he wasn't even two years old.' Hendrie agreed to join Todd's Middlesbrough on condition that he commuted to the ground, a round trip of 125 miles. He spent six seasons with them before joining Barnsley two years ago. 'I really like Barnsley,' said Linda. 'It's a down-to-earth place, where people aren't looking at what clothes you're wearing and that kind of thing. The players' wives have their own box at Oakwell and we are looked after really well.'

The erratic nature of a footballer's life has been distilled into the past few weeks for the Hendries. There was the elation of goals against Manchester United in the FA Cup, while injury has caused him to miss the quarter-final away to Newcastle and vital league wins against Wimbledon and Aston Villa. 'I was so proud of John after the United games,' said Linda. 'He is not so bad now when he is injured. He used to be highly strung when he was in his mid-twenties, a right little so and so at times. I knew he would mellow out as he got older.'

After a Saturday game, the family has the same routine and it is not infringed upon by football. 'John brings home a curry and we close the door and shut out the world. We never judge him or criticise him and the welcome he gets, especially from the younger kids, is always warm. We don't care whether Barnsley have won, lost or drawn.'

One national newspaper recently dubbed the liaison between David Beckham and his pop-singing fiancee as the 'romance of the decade'. When Posh Spice and Posh United have been together 16 years, endured and enjoyed four children, and moved countless times, the headlines might not seem quite so absurd. In the meantime, for the Hendries and scores of other journeymen professionals, the epithet is fitting.

---

*Saturday 14 March 1998*

**Barnsley 4 Southampton 3**

Barnsley edged an open game of flowing football. Ashley Ward, Scott Jones, Jan Aage Fjortoft and Neil Redfearn scored for Barnsley while Egil Ostenstad and Matt Le Tissier (two) replied for the visitors. It was Barnsley's third consecutive league win, their best form of the season, and it moved them to third from bottom.

The trio of centre backs, Adie Moses, Scott Jones and Chris Morgan were all products of Barnsley's youth system. It was the second consecutive game in which all three had played. Also in the team were David Watson, Nicky Eaden and Martin Bullock. Few Premiership teams could boast a team of which more than half was home-grown.

*Sunday 15 March 1998*

The squad flew out to Palma, Majorca, for a five-day break. 'The boys have been playing to their absolute maximum. It is important that we have some relaxation, mentally as well as physically,' said Danny Wilson. Andy Liddell, suffering from a broken nose, had to wear a mask to protect his face. As he made his way around the resort, he was serenaded constantly by team-mates singing songs from the *Phantom Of The Opera*. Jan Aage Fjortoft was the star turn on the karaoke – one of the team's favourite pastimes – running through various Stevie Wonder songs.

RIM KEEPS HIS FEET ON BARNSLEY'S GROUND
*(The Times, Saturday 21 March 1998)*

The cleaner puts down the handle of a vacuum cleaner and kindly offers to help. She pops her head into a room beneath

Barnsley's West Stand. 'Is Norman in there?' 'Yeah, he's under the table,' is the response. Good humour and Barnsley are best pals again – three consecutive league wins and a four-month unbeaten home record have seen to that.

While the first-team squad has spent this week relaxing in Spain, 74-year-old Norman Rimmington has chosen to remain at Oakwell. He has reserve matches away at Rotherham and Rochdale to occupy his thoughts. An apprentice, skin shining and hair floppy, sees him on the corridor. 'Rim, did those boots arrive, only I need them for tomorrow?' Almost everyone calls him 'Rim' or 'Rimmo'; it's the kind of nickname that schoolboys give to one another. Rimmington, a club stalwart for 55 years, is forever young.

During his time at the club he has been a goalkeeper, coach, assistant manager, groundsman, physiotherapist and, finally, kit manager. He sits in the boardroom during the interview, uneasy among the plush seats and wood-panelled walls. His real domain is the factory floor of Barnsley FC, the storerooms and dressing-rooms, where the air is heavy with the smell of boot polish and disinfectant and where, at every turn, there is a young face bidding: 'All right, Rim?'

By today's standards he does not seem tall enough for a goalkeeper, but he is thickset with large, gnarled hands. 'I would not choose to be a goalkeeper if I had my time again,' he said. 'When I played, you could get walloped and hammered. I've had my finger broken, my thumb, injured my leg, and I dislocated my shoulder in a game against West Brom.' He played 27 games for Barnsley before joining Hartlepool United for five seasons in 1946. He returned to his home town to work in the pits, from where he was summoned to coach Barnsley's A team and reserves.

In the early 1970s the club took a downturn, spending four seasons in the bottom half of the old Fourth Division. 'It was a very bad period,' said Rimmington. 'We were desperate for cash, the gates were down and we were having to perform miracles with players we'd got on free transfers. It seemed to be a losing battle. I got offers from other clubs but somehow or other, when you are from Barnsley, you do not want to leave.'

He settled on the perfect compromise when he left behind the despondency of the training ground to tend the Oakwell pitch. 'I just thought I'd have a bas'ı at being groundsman,' he said. 'I liked the fresh air and it took a lot of the pressure away. Looking after a pitch owes much to hard work and common sense.' In 1978, when the former Leeds United striker Allan Clarke joined as player-manager, Rimmington swapped jobs again. 'He wanted me to be the physio,' he said. 'I was enjoying doing the pitch but Allan doubled my wages. I didn't hesitate for long! Clarke led Barnsley to promotion in his first season, averaging almost a goal every three matches, and Rimmington believes he galvanised the club's dramatic change of fortune.

'He got the place buzzing,' said Rimmington. 'Everything seemed to boom when he was here and we didn't look back. I think Ernest [Dennis, Barnsley's late chairman] really pushed the boat out when he got Clarke. He forfeited his testimonial at Leeds to come here, so he must have been paid good wages.'

When Rimmington reached retirement, he told the club that he could no longer 'belt onto the field' to treat injured players. He was asked to become kit manager and accepted on one condition: 'I told them I didn't want to go to away matches. I'm pig sick of hotels. All you do is mooch around killing time. It's deadly.'

Kit manager is actually a misnomer as he is more of a personal valet to the legion of players, from the first team to the juniors, who wear the red of Barnsley. His inventory of responsibilities is long and meticulous. He must provide pre-match chocolate bars and chewing gum, cycle shorts of the optimum elasticity, tie-ups, football boots with various soles, training kit. He has a typed list of every player's idiosyncrasies.

After the interview he offers a quick tour of the various rooms beneath the stand. He opens the door to a tiny storeroom. 'I came in here on my own after the Bradford match when we won promotion,' he said. 'I just sat here for about half an hour and smoked a cigar.' In another windowless room, apprentices are scrubbing polish into boots. They smile and nod to him. There is life and vitality coursing through this football municipality and a perceptible respect for its elders. Danny Wilson and his young charges can enjoy their break in the sun. Barnsley FC is in safe hands. Safe gnarled hands.

---

A great deal was made during the season of the gamesmanship of Premiership teams. While Barnsley were slow to learn this technique of permissible on-field deceit, they had, down the years, already perfected their own brand of wile. The visitors' dressing room at Oakwell is tiny, a 5-a-side team would struggle to get changed and limber up in there without feeling overfamiliar with one another. The room is also directly above the boiler room, so the temperature is permanently high and the atmosphere stuffy.

Alex Ferguson and his team had stalled before entering this airless, claustrophobic box and, as far back as the first game of the season, West Ham's goalkeeper Ludek Miklosko had grumbled to reporters about the 'poor' facilities. At least the West Ham team had the benefit of running out on a warm sunny day. Others had to enter the ice-cold snap of a Yorkshire gale after sweltering in the dressing room. Many teams struggled in the first few minutes as they acclimatised themselves and it was no coincidence that Barnsley conceded fewer goals, on average, in the first 15 minutes than they did at any other period over the course of a match.

---

*Wednesday 25 March 1998*

Georgi Hristov scored the only goal of the game in Macedonia's victory against Bulgaria. Darren Barnard made his début for Wales in a 0-0 draw with Jamaica at Ninian Park. He was later teased by team-mates for his 'singing' during the national anthem; it was obvious that he did not know the words.

---

# LIFE AT THE TOP

## SMELLS LIKE TEAM SPIRIT AT OAKWELL
### (The Times, Saturday 28 March 1998)

Three beautiful girls step out of the longest car in London and ask their chauffeur to keep the engine running. They close the doors in slow motion and walk towards the café, all cheekbones and laughter. Ladbroke Grove is bathed in spring sunshine and the film crew is expected at any minute. Anton Brookes is in shades, loose-limbed among the lunch set, bidding a nonchalant hello to the soundtrack composer in the corner. The bill is put on the tab; he can pay next time, he's cool. He chooses a table on the pavement and in an accent that is a bizarre aggregate of Australian, West Coast America and South Yorkshire, enthuses about Barnsley FC. 'I kinda got into them in about 1973, I guess ... ' he begins.

In the grand fraternity of Barnsley supporters, Brookes is an enigma in a red-and-white scarf. While we can usually second-guess the occupation of the fan in the seat next to us, it might take extra time and penalties before we hit upon Brookes's vocation. 'I tell them I'm in the music business, or something really vague, like that I am working in London, and leave it at that. I rarely get asked, and it is hard to explain what a publicist does anyway,' he said.

Brookes is actually one of the most important players on the British music scene. He is one of the hidden manipulators, paid by record companies to ensure that their artists are widely and unequivocally recommended by music writers. He helped to propel Nirvana from a début album recorded for just $600 to *Nevermind*, which has sold 10 million copies and was recently dubbed 'the most profoundly influential LP of the decade' by *Q* magazine.

His company, Bad Moon Publicity, has colonised left-field music, from the Beastie Boys to Black Grape, Page and Plant to Smashing Pumpkins. While he has nurtured the most hip roster in pop, he has simultaneously conducted a love affair with Barnsley. 'Wherever I am in the world, I always put my Barnsley shirt up on the hotel wall. It is a karma thing, I suppose. I will always know the kick-off time in England and I visualise the game. It is my home town team, it could not be any other way,' he said.

Brookes takes on new groups by intuition; he trusts his ears and his heart and whether they remain obscure or become popular he will champion them steadfastly. In music terms, Barnsley were Carter the Unstoppable Sex Machine (a former Bad Moon client) who have suddenly gone Nirvana, or something like. If Brookes's name seems a tad showbiz, it is purely by accident. It was thrust upon him by classmates. In the mid-Seventies, Barnsley had a player called Anton Otulakowski, who later joined West Ham United. Since Anthony Brookes was forever talking about Barnsley, his name was shortened to Anton as a tribute to the midfield schemer.

He first attended Oakwell in September 1973 with his late father, Bill, a coal miner, and saw Barnsley draw 1-1 with Mansfield Town in the old Fourth Division. They were among a crowd of just 2,487, which illustrates the club's extraordinary upsurge in the past 25 years. 'I have been all over supporting them, places like Darlington, Plymouth and Scunthorpe,' he said. 'It doesn't seem all that long ago when we were going to those grounds. My Dad died five years ago and it was always his dream to see them in the Premiership. It was very emotional when we were promoted last season.' He had promised his Australian girlfriend, Tina, that they would marry if Barnsley won promotion, and they wed three months after the famous victory against Bradford City.

His professional life is organised largely around Barnsley's fixture list and this has meant the odd bizarre juxtaposition. 'I flew into Heathrow on a Saturday and drove straight to Bromsgrove where we were playing in the third round of the FA Cup. We won 2-1 and when the winner went in I was dancing on the pitch. I thought afterwards, "This is weird. I was in Santa Monica yesterday, looking at the Pacific Ocean."' Although he has lived in London for 15 years, he usually spends weekends in Barnsley when the team has a home match. 'Barnsley is very special, it is a unique place. People see it as a backwater, the land that time forgot, but it is not just full of meatheads,' he said. Glamour and Barnsley are hardly synonymous, though Brookes has brought to the club a tinge of rock'n'roll. He is happy to make modest statements by sponsoring a match ball or a player's kit. Andy Liddell, the Barnsley striker, has received the patronage of Bad Moon for the past four seasons, so this doyen of pop credibility shares match programme space with Blue Line Taxis, Blackburn's Cafe and Potters of Barnsley – award-winning pies and sausages. Brookes laughs at the irony, a twinkle beneath his shades. The beautiful girls return to the car, London swings, and all is well in Barnsley too.

---

*Saturday 28 March 1998*

**Barnsley 2 Liverpool 3**

A bunch of red-and-white roses were placed on the seat in the East Stand normally taken up by Nancie Pickard, a Barnsley season-ticket holder since 1930, who had died the previous Sunday. It was the only focus of calm on a strange, hostile afternoon.

---

DUBIOUS DECISIONS NO REASON TO PUT REFEREE IN JEOPARDY
*(match report, The Times, Monday 30 March 1998)*

The late attempt at dignity ended in pathetic fashion. Gary Willard, the match referee, held back his shoulders and marched confidently, defiantly towards the dressing rooms. Concealed within a phalanx of stewards and police – led, aptly enough, by a man in a white coat – the walk became hesitant as the first few objects were thrown. Phlegm and coins rained down viciously as they approached the West Stand. Eyes covered, they formed a protective scrum, and, finally, ran for their lives down the tunnel.

Afterwards, as sirens screamed and a lynch mob gathered in the streets, there was a sense of bewilderment. People wandered around dazed like road accident victims. Football, once more, had been reduced to a negligible side-issue, a piece of cheap theatre that had somehow tapped into the baseness of the human condition. On *Match of the Day* it was portrayed mendaciously, given a vaguely jovial touch – a 'Carry On Scrapping' to complement supper. In truth, it was an afternoon sheared raw, football beyond the edge of a nervous breakdown.

On a day when, elsewhere, a young supporter was stabbed to death in the name of the game, only a combination of heroism and good fortune spared us the sinister spectacle of seeing a referee set upon.

Gary Willard is a referee who plays the game literally by the book. Even before Saturday's game at Oakwell he had issued more yellow cards than any other Premiership referee, with 73 in just 16 matches. His early decisions were unfathomable, owing everything to pedantry and little to common sense. Babb lost his balance and collided with Marcelle. He was booked. Sheridan was a fraction late as he tackled Ince. He was booked. Matteo cynically drove his elbow into the back of Fjortoft. He was pardoned.

In between some enterprising play, several players unwittingly contributed to the game's slow detonation. McManaman picked a pointless fight with Barnard as they squabbled like schoolboys over a throw-in. Both McManaman and Ince were continually bleating to the referee, pointing to their shins and appealing for fouls. Redfearn scored for Barnsley and Riedle replied with a wonderful drive; in hindsight, it seems absurd to mention the actual football.

Barnard was sent off for tripping Owen, and a few minutes later Morgan collided with the same player and was also ordered from the field. The Barnsley support, which is renowned for treading the fine line between passion and hostility, was incensed. During the on-field squabbling that habitually follows a sending off, a fan raced on to the pitch and careered towards Willard. MacManaman swiftly side-stepped the intruder, but Fjortoft courageously wrestled the man to the ground. We were later to learn much of the bravery or otherwise of the players.

The rule of law had been lost and there was unrest at several points around the ground. The bond of trust between supporters and players was broken, the pitch no longer sacrosanct as they tried to break free of the ring of stewards. Amid the noise and confusion, Danny Wilson, the Barnsley manager, held his dignity, leaning on the dug-out, resplendent in a white shirt, rather like an office worker caught up in an excitable demo on his lunch break. Willard suddenly left the field, presumably to defuse matters, but it was too hot-wired, too out of control.

Willard returned after four minutes. Riedle scored and Redfearn equalised with a penalty before MacManaman scored with virtually the last kick of the game. Foolishly, he submitted himself to the Liverpool support behind the goal and this led to several arrests as they too invaded the pitch. As the players returned to their own halves, Willard again produced the red card, this time sending off Sheridan.

Fans spilled on to the pitch from all angles. Ince wrestled one to the floor and Redfearn stepped in between the referee and another. Thankfully, in the midst of anarchy there were still enough good men to uphold a vestige of probity. Shamefully, many Barnsley supporters applauded the pitch invaders as they were led away, though the desperate voice on the public address system was unequivocal: 'Ladies and gentlemen, please keep off the pitch. This is absolutely disgraceful.'

The managers dutifully attended the after-match press conference, as the sound of fury could be outside the ground. 'The ref lost the plot towards the end, but I do not want to give him the satisfaction of getting myself into trouble,' said Danny Wilson. 'I'm sure you know what I think but I can't say it.' Roy Evans, the Liverpool manager, said it had been a 'daft game'.

It was almost two hours after the game before police decided it was safe for Willard to leave the ground. On the long drive back to his home town of Worthing, this divorced father of two will have had more than enough time to ponder on the most fraught afternoon of his life. A referee, whatever the absurdity of his decisions, deserves the right of absolute safety, and he was not afforded this at Oakwell, far from it.

---

It was alleged after the game that some of the Liverpool players foolishly goaded the Barnsley supporters who had gathered around the team coach. It was dim-witted behaviour on an afternoon when emotions ran to such a pitch. A letter published in *When Saturday Comes* told of an incident involving Steve Harkness, the Liverpool defender. 'From the safety of the team bus, he rubbed thumb and forefinger together and informed the crowd of mainly kids that he had plenty of money,' wrote Edwin Pawlikow. 'When one of the parents unwisely got involved by stating that he too wasn't without, Harkness pretended to explode with mirth and pointed at the two kids' attire.'

Elsewhere, Liverpool supporters – who were not privileged enough to receive the same level of police protection as the team – found stones and bricks raining down upon them. Radio phone-in programmes received calls from visiting fans who had been forced to hurry away from Oakwell for their own safety.

---

*Tuesday 31 March 1998*

### Blackburn Rovers 2 Barnsley 1

A goal scored by Kevin Gallacher with just four minutes remaining robbed Barnsley of a point after Georgi Hristov had scored. Blackburn's first goal was scored by Martin Dahlin.

---

165

LIFE AT THE TOP

*Friday 3 April 1998*

The *Barnsley Chronicle* published 19 letters covering a whole broadsheet page from Barnsley supporters complaining about Gary Willard and, to a lesser degree, the antics of the Liverpool players.

———————

### HARSHEST LESSONS IN THE GAME OF LIFE
*(The Times, Saturday 4 April 1998)*

The prophecy is often uttered at football grounds. It is, of course, a euphemism. 'There's going to be a riot here,' they say, whenever the passion borders on hostility. At Oakwell last Saturday the euphemism was a truism. Gary Willard, the referee in charge of Barnsley's match against Liverpool, seemed to be a man tired of the banality of life, a man with an outlandish death wish.

In a game with nothing above the normal level of irascibility, he sent off three Barnsley players. If the reason for the dismissals was vague, there was nothing ambiguous about the actual procedure of sending them from the field. The cards were held up defiantly, victoriously almost, as if he was holding aloft a flag; a unique flag representing a nation of one. The body language was all wrong. There was no 'Sorry, son, had to do it', apologetic smile, or a shrug of the shoulders. It was showy, bloody-minded sternness, more of a 'Get off my pitch, you insolent fool'.

Willard chose precisely the wrong place to stage his three-card trick. Barnsley does not suffer fools and it has a historical mistrust of authority. While, like most clubs, Barnsley has undergone what sociologists call *embourgoisement* – you know, serviettes supplied with the pies, toilets that flush, fans that applaud David Seaman because he is the England goalkeeper, etc – there remains a mass of support based on fierce parochialism. They are ex-miners, and sons of ex-miners, once the aristocracy of the working class, now left with too much time on their hands to ponder Barnsley's next match. Back in the 1970s, they saw through the smoke and mirrors and detected that the National Coal Board had a secret agenda. They were patronised, told that too much time underground had made them over-fond of baseless conspiracy theories. In the 1980s the pits duly closed and their frustration was played out against lines of policemen.

The resentment, institutionalised now, still exists in Barnsley. The football club has become a focus for regional pride and naked passion; a two-fingered wave back to a country that they believe has consigned them to afternoon television and twice-weekly trips to the job club. Their nemesis arrived last weekend in the shape of a divorced father-of-two civil servant with a Saturday job as a football referee. There are 'honest' fouls in football – a clip of the heel, a shift of weight to slow up an opponent's run – and there are dishonest ones, too. Willard permitted the cynical, the puerile and the snide but gleefully punished the trivial. After this injustice had been reinforced beyond the point of tolerance, ill-feeling spread through Oakwell like a malignant Mexican wave. It was a grim irony that a banner bearing the word 'Justice' was held aloft by the Liverpool fans [this related to their plea for a further inquiry into the Hillsborough disaster].

The tension was more sinister and ugly than portrayed throughout this week. The death of a Fulham supporter and the various outbreaks of sports-related violence provided a cover for Barnsley. Willard was attacked from all angles and the game was eclipsed by another sick sport as police, stewards and players intercepted various beer-bellies on legs hurtling towards a seemingly impervious figure. Make no mistake, their plan was to do him serious harm and, without overplaying the drama, for a good while it looked as if the mob held the upper hand and we were to see Willard set upon.

The bravery of the players, Fjortoft, Ince and Redfearn in particular, was commendable. The Barnsley supporters who applauded the pitch invaders, however, deserved nothing but contempt. In the streets around Oakwell they screamed into television cameras that their club was being persecuted; Willard was a vindictive agent of the Premiership that wanted to relegate Barnsley and maintain its closed shop of big-city clubs. Their anger is understandable, even if their argument is specious. Barnsley have been good business for the Premier League. Their stirring battles with football's elite have made absorbing theatre. The fight against relegation has been a Rocky film transplanted to football. At one point they are flailing and helpless, then a string of wins, a spring in their step, and hope is renewed. Also, the Premier League would not be so gauche as to send Willard as the angel of death; it would, if it was driven by malevolence, draw the breath from the club surreptitiously without recourse to melodrama.

The combination of an abysmal refereeing display and a tempestuous Oakwell crowd was pretty much unique and should be viewed as such. A return to high perimeter fences, a deduction of points, or a hefty fine is an arbitrary punishment, hurting the majority for the few. Barnsley is what Barnsley is. If the goading is relentless and considered unfair, it will retaliate. The club can bring Premiership football to the town but it cannot instantly bring a saintliness and civility to the part of its community that seeks out martyrdom.

This is not to condone or canvass a metaphorical shrug of the shoulders, but a simple fact. All those that have this week lamented and squealed surprise that thuggery still exists within football are improvident. Hate, compassion and love are part of the human condition and sport is merely a reflection of life. Our best hope is that the balance falls most frequently on the side of compassion and love, and violent afternoons at Oakwell are rare; very rare.

———————

The supporter wrestled to the ground by Jan-Aage Fjortoft was Jared Ambler, a former soldier and an Oakwell regular since he was three years old. He was fined £400 at Barnsley Magistrates' Court and banned indefinitely from Oakwell by the club. In mitigation, he told the court: 'I cannot condone my behaviour.

I offer no excuses. The frustration and anxiety built up inside me by the way Barnsley Football Club have been treated this season and some of the refereeing decisions seemed so unfair.'

Danny Wilson was in favour of life-bans for fans who had encroached on to the pitch, and he took a fiercely personal perspective on events. 'We have worked our nuts off to try and stay in the top flight and the stupid antics of just a few idiots could undo it,' he said.

The sense of injustice and distress festered in Barnsley until the end of the season. It was impossible not to see the game as a turning point. The three players sent off were suspended afterwards and missed vital games, while the unsettling influence of the afternoon was manifest. In the final eight games of the season, Barnsley lost six, drew one, and won only one.

The nation, understandably, saw the incidents in isolation, while the Barnsley fans had the aggregate of a 'penalty' refused at Old Trafford in the FA Cup; a 'dive' by Dion Dublin losing them the match at Coventry City; Adie Moses's 'unfair' dismissal at Newcastle; and the leniency showed to Paolo Di Canio after he had repeatedly given verbal abuse to the linesmen and Gary Willard during their match against Sheffield Wednesday.

Malcolm Moyes, a Barnsley supporter, writing in the *Sheffield Star*'s football paper, the 'Green 'Un', distilled the feelings from the stands. 'Remember walking or driving home [after the Liverpool match], half-dazed, wondering why the most controversial and inept displays of officiating seem to have been in matches involving the Reds. Remember waking up the next day and being a little more cynical about a sport which seems to support through its closed-door inaction the most blatant anomalies.'

About 15 minutes into the Liverpool game, I vividly recall a thought I almost spoke aloud in the press box, but decided against, since no-one else seemed to sense anything. I nearly said something along the lines of, 'Is it me, or is this referee (his name was not important at this stage) giving everything to

Liverpool?' I thought better, and assumed my natural impartiality had wavered because of my affiliation to Barnsley. At that point, though, there had been no controversial decisions, but in the hurly-burly of the game it felt as if the referee was constantly favouring Liverpool.

In the weeks afterwards, the Barnsley supporters crackled with anger and frustration. It was a truism that Barnsley had garnered popular support because they were seen to play the game properly, without whingeing and bullying, and with a style of play that was bereft of the cynical and nasty. Despite this, they appeared to be penalised more severely than other teams who resorted to repugnant gamesmanship; indeed, this clandestine cheating appeared part of their game plan.

Apart from Willard's eccentric performance – which was conceivably enough in itself – there was perhaps a rationale to the other decisions which fostered such antipathy in Barnsley. As members of the Premiership, Barnsley, for the first time ever, were subject to comprehensive television filming. Every incident was replayed constantly and commented upon; perceived injustices were exaggerated and given a profundity that their supporters had never known before.

Meanwhile, decisions from which Barnsley benefited were disregarded, and passed by unnoticed. This is in the nature of the football supporter, they will talk endlessly about the penalty that should have been, and spend less than a minute to acknowledge that their second goal should have been disallowed because the striker was a mile offside.

So, there was no persecution, nothing untoward, just a bunch of people rallying to an old song of injustice. Why, then, after 15 minutes of the game, did it feel as if something very peculiar was happening?

# CHAPTER NINE

## God in a Tracksuit

*Saturday 4 April 1998*

## Leeds United 2 Barnsley 1

Barnsley had their fourth player sent off in three games when Georgi Hristov twice swore at the referee's assistant, Eddie Walsh. He had earlier equalised after Jimmy Floyd Hasselbaink had scored for Leeds. Barnsley lost a drab match when Adie Moses inadvertently headed into his own goal. 'Their application was zilch,' complained Danny Wilson afterwards. He was similarly direct on Hristov's sending off. 'It was absolutely stupid. It cost us the match.'

After the game, 16 Barnsley fans were arrested when trouble flared in Wakefield town centre.

———————

### BLOWING THE WHISTLE ON A LOST SENSE OF HUMOUR
*(The Times, Saturday 11 April 1998)*

A neatly typed agenda was handed to everyone attending the monthly meeting of the Barnsley Supporters' Club. It remained unread, left on chairs, or tucked into coat pockets; everyone knew the night's business anyway. Barnsley fans are still simmering about the performance of Gary Willard, the referee who officiated at the 3-2 home defeat against Liverpool when three of their players were sent off. While their anger was once naked and hostile, it is now tempered with reason, and not a little humour. A shopkeeper in the town has stuck a poster in his window: 'Body parts shrunk to order. Premier League referees done free.'

The guest speakers on Thursday evening were, aptly enough, two Premiership referees, Uriah Rennie and Steve Lodge. Since they are both from Yorkshire – regional loyalty even runs to a pride in its own referees – and, more pertinently, ineligible to referee Barnsley league games, their reception was more cordial than might have been expected. If the agenda had mentioned a G Willard from Worthing the beer would have been served in plastic glasses.

'He should not be allowed near Oakwell for a very, very long time. If ever,' said one fan. 'Paul Ince made more decisions than he did,' complained another. 'The guy was appalling and there is quite clear evidence that we are sick of it,' said a voice at the back. Although there is obvious dismay about the sendings-off, the main tenet of supporters' anger is a perceived injustice. 'They are frightened to death of booking internationals and all these famous players, frightened to death,' was the summary of one fan. Barnsley on a chilly spring night is some prospect, but compound it with a foaming discontent, and a mistrust of anyone on merely nodding terms with Willard of Worthing, and one might expect a simpering telephone call two hours before the meeting: 'This sniffle has turned into quite a bad cold, Mr Chairman ... ' Not so. Step forward, Rennie and Lodge. The names already have the genial zing of a comedy double act and when the nefarious world of big-time football has no more use for these men, they should be booked immediately on a theatre tour of Britain's seaside towns.

They arrived resplendent in freshly-ironed blazers and fairly gambolled into the room. Lodge, hair combed forward, looked as if he had been dressed and groomed by his mother for his first day at school. He has the shy, understated demeanour of a schoolboy, but also that famous withering stare exclusive to Yorkshiremen. Their mouths stay shut, but the pinched, pained expression says: 'Tha's a pillock, and tha probably knows it too.' Rennie is all smiles and charm, the Eric Morecambe to Lodge's Ernie Wise. He rolls his shoulders, tosses back his head. He praises Barnsley on its quota of good-looking women and asks for more ladies to ask questions. He jokes about his footballing skills: 'I was quality. Do you remember Socrates, the Brazilian midfielder? I modelled myself on him.' Only once does the smile leave his face, when he is asked yet again about Willard. 'I am not the PR guy for our friend down south,' he says. Subject closed.

A supporter had heard a rumour about big clubs and their, hmmm, special relationship with referees. 'I've heard that they meet you at the motorway, give you a chauffeur driven ride to your hotel ... ' He wants to list the other wonderful acts of kindness, but is interrupted by Lodge. 'You'll be saying they give us a little brown envelope next, won't you?' he says. 'A big brown envelope would be better,' laughs Rennie. 'Is that taxable though?' counters Lodge. At this point, Supporters' Club officials are scanning the top table for the duo's scripts. For the record, Rennie had to make his own cup of tea during a recent visit to Old Trafford; so much for championship hospitality.

Rennie confirmed that managers were sometimes aggressive towards referees when out of sight of the pitch. 'They come down the corridor shouting F- words and kicking doors. I tell them to go away and cool down and then come back later. I will not have anyone coming in my dressing room belittling me,' he said.

Several Barnsley supporters expressed surprise that Georgi Hristov had been sent off for swearing against Leeds United last week. 'I thought he couldn't speak English,' pondered one. An explanation was at hand. 'He only knows two words, and the second is "off".' David Mellor, the host of Radio Five Live's phone-in programme, *Six O Six*, was also implicated in the conspiracy theories that have beset Barnsley. 'He only let a few people from Barnsley speak after the Liverpool game,' someone grumbled. 'He's a prat anyway,' consoled another.

There is, evidently, a smile back on the face of Barnsley, even if it is a smile in crisis. They are determined that Willard should be answerable for his actions, and are planning a thoughtful, considered campaign. They are aware that too much hostility and whingeing, and one too many conspiracy theories, could hinder their progress. They should borrow Rennie's good humour, Lodge's pragmatism, and see what fate brings.

---

*Saturday 11 April 1998*

### Barnsley 2 Sheffield Wednesday 1

Despite dominating the play, Barnsley took over an hour to score. Ashley Ward collected a long throw-in from Krizan and turned it past Kevin Pressman for his 10th goal of the season. Jan-Aage Fjortoft increased the lead before Dejan Stefanovic set up a nervous finish, scoring five minutes before the end.

It was Barnsley's last win in the Premiership. Their closing five games included four defeats and a draw, with only two goals scored.

———————

*Monday 13 April 1998*

## Newcastle United 2 Barnsley 1

Andreas Andersson, Newcastle's recent signing from AC Milan, scored his first goal for the club but Jan-Aage Fjortoft equalised when a Ward shot ricocheted from Shay Given. Fjortoft collided with the post when scoring and was taken off injured. Alan Shearer scored a headed winner with five minutes remaining. Arjan de Zeeuw claimed he had been pushed by the England captain as the ball was crossed into the penalty area.

———————

LIVING CHRONICLE RENOWNED FOR LETTING OTHERS HAVE FINAL WORD
*(The Times, Saturday 18 April 1998)*

Fast legs and a keen heart were not quite good enough; Colin Smallman and Wilf Lingard knew as much. Out in front was Benny Hill, small and skinny, and determined to win. The *Barnsley Chronicle* duly recorded the moment: 'Darfield Council School, Obstacle Race (Senior Boys) 1. B. Hill, 2. C. Smallman, 3. W. Lingard.'

The tiny cutting has turned from white to ochre during the 57 years it has remained in Hill's scrapbook. Only Hill would have cared enough to cut and mount the news item. This is a man with an obsessive, compulsive personality, the king of the anoraks, would he wear anoraks that is, since stripy blazers are more his line.

Puff of the pipe, slight tilt of the head, sideways smile, Hill can tell you anything you need to know about Barnsley Football Club, tha knows. And some more. He has kept meticulous details about every game played since the 1938-39 season and has at least one report on every Barnsley match since 1953. 'My mother used to say I was born with a pen in my hand. It's the way I am, an organiser,' he says.

Despite his love of minutiae, Hill is hardly the austere bureaucrat. The eyes twinkle behind his glasses, and once he sets upon a tale, it will be peppered with humour and blunt opinion, not to mention the odd swear word or two. After Barnsley's fraught match against Liverpool three weeks ago, the tension in the press room was unbearable. Danny Wilson entered and the press corps stared down nervously at the floor. Suddenly, Hill spoke everyone's thoughts. 'That referee [Gary Willard], what a pillock, eh Danny?' Wilson – three of his players sent off, the team defeated, fans going berserk – broke into a pirate smile. The anxiety left the room, life went on.

Hill is granted access to press facilities partly as a thank you for the column 'Stop Press' which has appeared in Barnsley's match programme since 1974. The column is a 400-word bulletin from a journalist specially invited to write a piece by Hill. By the end of this season nearly 300 writers will have contributed 250,000 words of copy – none of them paid. 'Aye, they've all done it for nowt, and in all that time only two have asked for payment. I'm mentioning no names though,' he says.

The list of contributors is a who's who of British sports reporting, from John Motson to Brough Scott, Jimmy Armfield to Jon Champion, Eleanor Oldroyd to Martin Tyler. One notable omission has been Barnsley's most famous son of the pen, Michael Parkinson. 'I'll get that bugger to do me a piece one day,' says Hill.

Journalists are willing to offer their services freely as a response to Hill's unwavering enthusiasm and also because he is 'one of them'. He is a former sports editor of the *Barnsley Chronicle* and the now-defunct *Sheffield Morning Telegraph*. He is proud that not a single day of his working life was spent outside newspapers. He covered his first Barnsley match in October 1948, a 4-0 defeat at Coventry City, and by 1974 he had filed copy from all 92 grounds of the Football League.

He is not without his idiosyncrasies, which is a polite way of saying he has an opinion, and here it comes, bombast tempered with good humour. 'Players who don't have a shave get my goat. I don't like these lazy buggers who will not shave. West Ham used to come to Oakwell looking really smart. They might have looked like spivs from London, but that's another story. Anyway, they came here at the start of the season and they looked like a set of bloody gardeners.'

Modern coaches that over-complicate football are next in line. 'It's a simple, dramatic game. We don't want to see players like McManaman running back and tackling people in the right-back position,' he says.

The eyes burnish some more as he talks of journalism and 'my lads', the term he uses for colleagues and acquaintances that have graduated from local papers to a certain amount of national eminence. 'John Motson was one of ours. He was as green as a fresh apple when I knew him, but he listened and wanted to learn.' Currently, two of the *Morning Telegraph*'s old boys are running the sportsdesks at *The Sun* and the Press Association.

He concedes that Barnsley's survival prospects are 'looking grim' but he has not yet abandoned hope. 'I ain't given up yet. I know we're hanging by a thread, but I'm not giving up.' Although he has a gratis press-box seat, it is only on a timeshare basis. When he sits down in seat E8 against Tottenham Hotspur today, he will first have to wipe away a significant amount of bird droppings. 'There's this pigeon and it's always sitting above the seat dropping its load on to it. It's getting to something isn't it when the pigeons are also getting nervous?'

---

*Friday 17 April 1998*

The forthcoming game against Tottenham Hotspur was billed as a relegation decider. They were just two points in front of

Barnsley, for whom a win would have lifted them out of the relegation zone. 'This is the big one. This is the game we have to win,' said Danny Wilson. Keith Lodge, writing in the *Barnsley Chronicle*, was moved to pen some impassioned prose as he rallied support for the team: 'Let them know they'll never walk alone; that you love them; that there's only one Danny Wilson; and you're still walking in a Wilson wonderland.'

---

*Saturday 18 April 1998*

### Barnsley 1 Tottenham Hotspur 1

An early goal by Neil Redfearn failed to inspire Barnsley and they conceded an equaliser by Colin Calderwood two minutes into the second half. Tottenham's erratic defender, Ramon Vega, was sent off for holding back Ashley Ward, but the visitors still held firm.

The Barnsley players left the pitch slowly with their heads down, almost as if they sensed that relegation was closing in.

---

### THE LANCASHIRE LAD WHO GREW ON BARNSLEY
*(The Times, Saturday 25 April 1998)*

The matchday attire is strictly formal – club blazer, club tie, white shirt, smart trousers. During the week, he prefers a training top and a pair of shorts. Stitched into the cloth is 'DW', but 'GOD' might be more appropriate.

Danny Wilson walks on water. To suggest otherwise in the pubs, clubs or supermarkets around Barnsley, or certain parts of Lancashire, is to summon a lynch mob to your door. Aside from being a god in a tracksuit, he may soon find himself declared a 'piece of public art'. A campaign is under way to erect a statue of him in Barnsley town centre. 'What he has done for the town is unbelievable,' said Alan Bloore, chairman of the Barnsley Supporters' Club. 'He has transformed the place, put us on the map. I think something should be done like this, why not?'

During Barnsley's fraught season, Wilson's composure has marked him out as a man of integrity. There has been no petulance or pettiness. In the heat of battle, he has loosened his collar, mustered a half-smile, and spoken candidly, but without rancour. He does not have the vaudevillian charisma, of, say, a Ron Atkinson, but possesses a charm of his own. It is understated, considered, and his gaze meets yours – unflinchingly, incisively. Most of all, he is admired because he is perceived as being true to himself.

Of course, before a throng of notebooks, or amid the glow of television lights, there are a few seconds of contemplation, a chance to loosen up the muscles clinging to hot-wired bones. On the eve of a crucial league game, however, when your sister has just called to say a reporter is snooping around your home-town, the emotions are raw, and the words trip over themselves wantonly.

'Are you the person asking for information about Danny Wilson?' he asked. I recognised the voice immediately. 'Is that you, Danny?'

We had met up a few weeks earlier and 'clicked' immediately, talking about football long after the allotted interview time. I explained that my motives were wholesome, it was merely research for this column, nothing sinister or traitorous. The *Wigan Evening Post* had carried a short news item to help round up some of Wilson's pals from his days as a young footballer. His manner was aggressive, perhaps understandably so; someone, without his knowledge, was – as he saw it – raking through private matters.

I phoned him several times the following week, but my calls were not returned. I sent him a conciliatory letter, apologising for the misunderstanding. Eventually, I received a two-line note: 'I have no power to stop you doing anything you wish if you feel it will make good reading, it is entirely your decision.' It was a dearth of words, and, it appears, the death of a nascent friendship. It was perfunctory, not hinting at forgiveness, or reconciliation.

Ironically, the response to my appeal brought forth a thunderous song of praise. The boy done well, and their pride is writ large across Lancashire. He is decent and moral, trustworthy, and loyal to his roots. He has crossed no-one. Ever. Until now.

Wilson is cut from the same rough stone as the managerial greats of British football. He was born to working-class parents, Jim and Annie Wilson, who settled in Billinge, Lancashire, after Jim left the Royal Navy to work as a forklift truck driver. 'Danny wasn't born with a silver spoon in his mouth, far from it,' said Mike Taylor, the former secretary of Wigan Amateur League. 'There has never been anyone holding his hand, he has had to fend for himself. His parents loved him, but they didn't mollycoddle him.'

As a teenager, Wilson played for the League's representative side and Taylor remembers calling for him one morning. 'He was still in bed. When he came to the door half-awake, I said "What's your game, Danny?" He grabbed his muddy boots and we set off,' he said. 'I see him now and I think he is the smartest-looking manager in the Premier League, speaking in measured tones. He has done well because he has the brains to listen and learn and soak it all up.'

David Denner played alongside him for Billinge FC. 'He was very mature for his age. He would gee people up, help them out if they were having a bad time,' he said. 'He was so good that he became a marked man and took some stick with people trying to chop him down. I cannot recall him ever losing his temper though.'

Sunderland signed Wilson on associate schoolboy forms but did not offer him an apprenticeship because they felt he was too small. 'He was very, very disappointed,' said Brian Hughes, the coach of Double Seven Youth Club for whom he also played. 'He didn't get too down though, he wasn't that type of lad. He never complained. Although he was a brilliant player, he never moaned to the other lads if they hadn't done so well.'

Hughes worked as a cheese wholesaler – 'Lancashire cheese, mainly', he says with pride – and the team sometimes travelled to matches in his van. Another mode of transport was on the back of a coal wagon, when Wilson played for Birchley St Mary's on Sunday afternoons. 'He roughed it with the rest of us. He was very small and unassuming, but he would take on players who were much bigger than him without a second thought,' said Eric Littler, the team's manager.

After leaving school, Wilson joined his father at Ravenhead brickworks; friends sensed that he was disillusioned about a career in the professional game. Geoff Kearsley, another Billinge FC player, was driving home one evening when he caught sight of Wilson. 'It was absolutely bucketing down and I saw this hunched figure with a haversack on his back. I remember him saying, "There's no way I'm doing this for the rest of my bloody life." He was a professional at Bury within six months,' he said.

Before joining Bury, Wilson played briefly for Wigan Athletic, but after just seven full appearances, he joined Bury. He had a nomadic playing career, turning out for seven clubs before arriving at Oakwell from rivals Sheffield Wednesday in the close season of 1993. 'He was the most hated man in Barnsley when he first came,' said Alan Bloore. 'They used to boo when his name was read out over the Tannoy. They would shout "Get back to Wednesday". But he stuck at it, his form improved, and he won people over.'

Some of his friends have been surprised to see a reserved personality develop a flinty sheen of self-confidence. Others, though, have recognised the influence of two decades in the game. 'He's never been in any other industry. He knows it back to front,' said Kearsley. 'He knows which players are with him and the ones who are peeing up his back.' One senior Barnsley player hinted at a firmness, an unequivocal self-belief that is vital for managerial success. 'Aye, Danny will let you have your say, but you'll still have to do it his way all the same!' he said.

———————

The first draft of this article did not contain any mention of Wilson's phone call to me. It was a straight, uncritical piece, another eulogy in a season of many. I wondered if I had made too much fuss about his call back in January. Had I been far too sensitive, should I have shrugged my shoulders and not given it a second thought?

An hour after I had filed the copy, Keith Blackmore, deputy sports editor at *The Times*, called and said something along the lines of, 'This is all well and good, but we know more about Wilson than you're letting on, don't we?' He did not insist that I mention the incident, but thought it germane to the feature. After a few hours thought, I was glad he had made the call, glad to defend my own integrity. In the slim likelihood of Wilson reading it, I did not want him to feel that he could treat someone so poorly (the outburst I could excuse, but not the token, meaningless response to my apology) and still find himself venerated in an article bearing my name.

My first loyalty was to the truth and the feature was purposely written in a non-judgmental way, allowing the readers to make up their own minds. I told of his popularity with others, and was prepared to stand alone as, it would appear, the only person to have had an altercation with him.

I was due to cover Barnsley's game against Arsenal on the day of publication and realised there was a chance I might be singled out by Wilson at the press conference after the game. I also knew that football people were notoriously forgetful of faces, and names.

---

*Saturday 25 April 1998*

**Barnsley 0 Arsenal 2**

The PFA Player of the Year, Dennis Bergkamp, scored in the first half and another Dutch international, Marc Overmars, increased the lead 14 minutes before the end. Arsenal, champions-to-be, were a class apart. Survival was still mathematically possible for Barnsley, but extremely unlikely.

---

# GOD IN A TRACKSUIT

## WENGER SAVOURS SPECIAL ARSENAL VINTAGE
### (match report, The Times, Monday 27 April 1998)

The timing was impeccable, which is only customary these days when it involves Arsenal. Their manager, Arsène Wenger, picked his way courteously through journalists in the press room at Oakwell. On a television set perched just a few feet above him, Frank McLintock, the captain of Arsenal's exalted team of the early Seventies, was conducting a homage to the current incumbents.

For a few long seconds, no-one could find the remote control. In the small cramped room, Arsenal were suddenly everywhere; in front, behind, above, past, present, and, most likely, future.

When Barnsley secured promotion to the Premiership exactly a year ago to the day, it was their dream to share pitch space with footballing dynasties like Arsenal. They occupied the same space on Saturday, but they were incorporeal, mere wisps of ragged red smoke, drifting aimlessly between the white outlines of the playing area.

Their big hearts and big lungs kept the scoreline respectable, but they were outclassed all the same. Their supporters were magnanimous enough to·concede the fact and applauded both the Arsenal side and their fans at the final whistle. There was even a rousing cheer of 'Champions' from the Ora Stand, which houses the most vociferous section of Barnsley's support. Respect indeed.

The Arsenal family tradition has always been to place opponents in a metaphorical headlock, before breaking free to sneak an infamous 1-0 win. In short, they bored a game to death and laughed all the way back to Highbury. Wenger, a coach with a draftsman's eye for detail, has maintained the shellac-coated defence, but added a touch of rococo in players like Bergkamp and Overmars.

They both scored against Barnsley and it was appropriate because they exemplified the contrast in the teams, between the brilliant and the mediocre, the gifted and the also-ran. The pair are typical of many superlative players; they can appear disinterested, lost in reverie, for long periods and suddenly jolt into life. Where, just a few seconds earlier, they were all but chatting with fans at the fence or counting blades of grass, they are now tearing remorselessly through a defence, and the ball is heading undeviatingly for the back of the net.

Barnsley started well and repelled the visitors for 25 minutes, which almost ranks as a moral victory while Arsenal are in such blistering form. Bergkamp was lingering a few yards outside the Barnsley penalty area when forced into the game by Petit. De Zeeuw and Eaden were within a yard of him, but they might as well have been in the car park collecting their coats. He swivelled, accelerated like a Ferrari between two souped-up Minis, and the ball was in the net. Game over.

Desperate for points for league survival, Barnsley maintained an impressive work-rate. Redfearn, as ever, conducted the toil, but he received only nominal support from Tinkler and Bullock around him. Fjortoft was slow and cumbersome and, even with Ward alongside him after half-time, this heavyweight attack was swatted like pesky flies by Adams and Keown.

Arsenal threatened to increase their lead several times, but 14 minutes before the end it was another Ferrari versus Mini road race as Overmars zipped through Barnsley's rearguard. The ball evaded the right hand of a diving Watson and nestled, with a certain inevitability, in the back of the net. The Arsenal backroom team, not a group of men prone to showy emotion, leapt from the dug-out as if their bench had been wired to the mains. The goal had secured the win that, surely now, had secured the championship.

Barnsley, in order to survive, have to win their two remaining games against Leicester City and Manchester United, and hope that others around them lose. If they are defeated at Filbert Street on Saturday they will be relegated. 'It is a tall order,' said Danny Wilson. 'But we are still in there fighting. We haven't given up yet.' He was keen to praise Arsenal: 'They are a class act, simple as that. They controlled the game, in all honesty, and played it at their own pace. They are going to take some stopping now.'

Arsène Wenger had recovered his usual composure after the touch-line animation, and was reflective, as if he saw the impropriety of jigging at another club's wake. 'The Barnsley players gave everything today and you could not reproach any of them. It is a shame that they may now be relegated, because it has not given them enough time to learn from their mistakes,' he said.

If he has mastered the peculiarities and complexities of English football, he has also learned the value of a sound-bite. 'He scores only best-sellers,' he responded, when asked about Bergkamp's goal. He smiled, he knew the line was awful really, comically awful – just what was required. Clever man, clever team.

———————

I was approached at half-time and full-time by a handful of journalists empathising with my piece on Wilson. I imagined that they would consider I had broken ranks, even though the copy was delicate and circumspect. After all, Wilson was marked down as a good guy; solid and trustworthy, and I had suddenly become a dissident.

A couple said they had been involved in squabbles with Wilson over essentially trivial matters, where they had been astonished that he had reacted in such a way over 'something or nothing'. They had not written anything negative about Wilson because it was imperative that they remained on friendly terms for on-going stories emanating from Oakwell; this is the reason why much sports journalism is bloodless and dreary. Referees and FA officials, for example, receive constant broadsides because they have no powers of retaliation, while footballers and managers are sacrosanct.

The Supporters' Club officials, who I had forewarned about the piece, were cordial when we met up before the match. 'It seemed fair enough to me,' said Alan Bloore. They did not feel I had been unfair to Wilson or that I had acted duplicitously. One fan, however, over-hearing our conversation, butted in with the remark: 'Danny asked you not to write anything, but you still went ahead, didn't you?' I told him it was my first duty to write the truth. He looked at me with utter disgust in his eyes.

# LIFE AT THE TOP

CHAPTER TEN

A Wake of Sorts

## Young Blood Reviving Club Where Hope Ails
*(The Times, Saturday 2 May 1998)*

No-one had really noticed him. He might have been queueing at the tea hut for all the influence he was having on the game. Abruptly, he was drawn into the play. A swivel of the hips, a sudden acceleration, one-nil to the Ar-se-nal.

For a ghastly minute, it reminded the Barnsley faithful of the bad old days of about four months ago, when their beloved team would trudge around, cement in their boots, while the lithesome sprats from Big Time FC effortlessly notched yet another goal;  6-0, and the big Oakwell oh no.

Dennis Bergkamp and a handful of his colleagues were, quite simply, in a league of their own last Saturday. Not for the first time this season, it marked out the distance between Barnsley and football's elite, the dilettante and the dynasty. Tactics and toil are sometimes enough, but worthless against players with magic feet.

Arsenal are the quintessential football empire, a club imbued with tradition, organisation, thoroughness. When players pull on the red and white shirt they sense its importance and their absolute privilege. They are part of a kinship, and of the age when it is their turn to wear the family colours.

The immediate prognosis for Barnsley is not good and they will be relegated if they do not win at Leicester City today. While their Premiership pulse is faint, the club has made, by its own standards anyway, a prodigious investment in its long-term future. It does not want to merely share pitch space with the Arsenals and Manchester Uniteds, it aspires to its own perpetuity of quality, a Kwiksave with designs to become a Marks and Spencer.

Barnsley's starting line-up against Arsenal included four players who have been associated with the club since they were schoolboys. Chris Morgan, another to have worked his way through the ranks, would have taken his place among the back three had he not been suspended.

The town has a long tradition of producing players of a high standard. Barnsley Boys have won the English Schools Trophy outright on three occasions and this year shared it with Bristol and South Gloucester Boys. Among a long list of professionals to graduate from the team are Tommy Taylor, Alan Woodward, Frank Casper, Jimmy Greenhoff, Pat Howard and Stewart Barraclough. Barnsley FC's vice-chairman, Barry Taylor, was captain of the Barnsley Boys team which shared the trophy with Southampton in 1957, when the Oakwell leg of the final was played before a crowd of more than 19,000.

Three full-time members of staff are charged with ensuring that Barnsley's success is not ephemeral. Colin Walker, Peter Casken, and Maurice Firth are youth team coach, academy director and youth liaison officer respectively. Like many clubs, Barnsley is about to launch its own academy of football. The terminology might be a tad cumbersome, but the aim is direct enough – find young players, nurture them, and supply them primed for the first team.

'The word I always use when asked what we are looking for in a lad is attitude,' said Maurice Firth, who has been connected with Barnsley for more than 40 years. 'Attitude' is his shorthand for determination, loyalty, a willingness to learn, a love of the club. 'Technically, the lads are sound. They can do those Cruyff turns in their sleep, but their attitude has got to be just right,' he said.

The progress of Chris Morgan has been a fillip to the back-room staff. He is seen as epitomising the spirit of the club. 'The first time he saw me after he had broken into the first team, he came over and shook my hand. He said, "Thanks a lot." It was only a small thing in itself, but it made me feel good,' said Firth.

Next season Barnsley will have representative teams from under-nines to under-16s. At the age of 16, players with first-team potential will be offered a three-year scholarship at the club which effectively replaces the old apprenticeship scheme. Each week they are guaranteed 12 hours of football coaching and 12 hours of education.

There is a well-spring of talent in the South Yorkshire area, but the competition for young players is intense, with a certain level of venality involved in their acquisition. 'Put it this way,' said Firth, 'There are some clubs, not naming any names, who we will not play friendly matches against for obvious reasons. I tell my scouts not to approach lads signed for other clubs. They should make a note of their details, just in case they become free at a later date.'

Money does change hands illegally in some cases, but most inducements are more subtle and covert. A potential new signing might be invited on a tour of Holland with the youth squad, and, hey, mum and dad are welcome too.

Barnsley cannot promise huge salaries, or even national fame, but Colin Walker takes special bait when he visits the home of a promising schoolboy. 'I sometimes take a first team shirt, and I say, "If you're good enough and you work hard enough, this is yours in a few year's time." They look at our first team and see the likes of Morgan, Eaden, Watson, and I think it gives them hope that they can make it.'

Walker knows more than anyone about the zeal with which clubs pursue talented schoolboys. He was himself a footballing child prodigy, scoring 166 goals during one season of just 22 games. He was featured on national television and dubbed 'Better Than George Best' by one newspaper. He was slow to develop physically and while he was coveted by football's gentry at the age of 10, the interest in a 15 year-old just 5 ft 1 in tall was nominal. Still, after a growth spurt, he eked out a living in the game, from Matlock Town to Sheffield Wednesday, taking in several lower-league professional teams and a spell as an international for New Zealand, after he emigrated there in he 1980s.

Like most of Barnsley's boot room team, including Danny Wilson who worked in a brick works, Walker has served time as a 'civvy'. He was a dustman for three years, and he brings this slice-of-life authenticity to his dealings with young players. He was also a Barnsley player, with a commendable strike rate of 12 goals in 24 matches. 'He was crap, but he could score goals – and I always tell him that too,' said John Dennis.

Some believe that Barnsley's dream of a sovereignty based

upon gilded youth will flounder alongside their Premiership existence. 'It's all very expensive to set up, and it may become a white elephant if they don't have success with the first-team,' said one insider. True, but Barnsley is a club that does not spend what it does not have, nor say what it does not mean. Noticeably, from chairman to scout, it is currently talking in most un-Yorkshire terms about its burgeoning youth set-up.

*Saturday 2 May 1998*

### Leicester City 1 Barnsley 0

A goal by Leicester City's Greek international, Theo Zagorakis, sealed victory in a dull, lifeless match. At 4.50 pm Barnsley were relegated officially from the Premiership. A win would not have made matters any different because Tottenham Hotspur and Bolton Wanderers, their relegation rivals, recorded wins against Wimbledon and Crystal Palace respectively.

Dickie Bird was umpiring a match between Sussex and Hampshire when the score was relayed to him. 'It left me feeling numb and shocked,' he said. He was consoled by the Hampshire captain, Robin Smith.

Many Barnsley fans travelled back to Oakwell after the game to greet the players as they disembarked from the team coach.

*Sunday 3 May 1998*

Ashley Ward was awarded the Supporters' Club Player of the Year trophy at their annual function at Oakwell. Chris Morgan was chosen as Young Player of the Year. Barnsley have four distinct player of the year awards and Ashley Ward won each of them. Aside from the Supporters' Club award, there is the Supporters' Player of the Year, voted for by fans not necessary members of the Supporters' Club; the club's Player of the Year chosen by a panel including Danny Wilson; and the Disabled

Supporters' Player of the Year. In the supporters' poll – which is perhaps most in touch with the club's grass roots following – Ward polled more than the double the votes for the runner-up, Neil Redfearn, who pipped David Watson to second place by one vote.

---

BARNSLEY FINALLY BOW OUT TO THE INEVITABLE
*(match report, The Times, Monday 4 May 1998)*

### Leicester City 1 Barnsley 0

The large man in a thick overcoat was flanked by two stewards. At the final whistle, he walked slowly and reluctantly around the edge of the pitch, invisible bricks around his feet, an invisible brick in his heart.

When the television people set about him with their blazing lights at Filbert Street on Saturday, he managed to rouse a semblance of fighting talk. Since his is an unfamiliar face, the strapline was provided: 'John Dennis, Barnsley chairman.' 'Its been a wonderful experience, just to be a part of the Premiership ... ' he began. He has learnt to put on a good show, to focus on the positive and talk it up for a microphone.

'Is this off the record?' he will ask later in a quiet corner of a quiet room. The trusted few will then hear the real truth – for there are several versions – about the relegation of Barnsley back to football's hinterland. He will talk, in refreshingly plain terms, of the disappointment, the frustration, the anger.

This is a football club chairman of the old school. A fanatic who just happens to have a larger bank balance than your average supporter. His father, Ernest Dennis, was chairman before him, and John Dennis has been connected with the club for more than 40 years. When Barnsley lose, staff at Oakwell keep out of his way because one of his sulks can last from Saturday to Wednesday. It will take him most of the summer to recover from relegation.

As he made his way across the cinders, the Barnsley

supporters housed on the other side of the pitch sang victoriously in defeat, that they were staying put, not going home. Their home is a different place now their team has given them pride and fame. The fans were, in effect, celebrating each other, a town united by football. Where Barnsley was once perceived as grimy and unrefined, the football team has added a semblance of sophistication, a dash of glamour.

Portentously, a sun that had sent dazzling patterns over the nearby River Soar became pale and indifferent at the kick-off. It was an overcast game of tired legs and lazy minds, between teams all played out. August to May has been a long journey for players who, in the main, are forced to rely on exuberance more than enterprise. They played similar tactical formations and, like two people continually bumping into each other in a narrow corridor, there was nowhere to move, no way out.

Much has been made of Barnsley's improvement in the second half of the season, but their form in recent weeks has been poor; they have not looked like a Premiership side. Their passing has disintegrated and their celebrated spirit and endeavour have been hard to discern in the final run-in of eight games, which has included six defeats. Against Leicester, Neil Redfearn, their captain and best player in adversity, was often caught in possession and his lack of pace and incision summarised the team's malaise.

Leicester stirred themselves enough to create a goal 12 minutes into the second half. Guppy's cross was turned into the path of Zagorakis, who poked it home without conviction. The goal secured a win that will be vital if Leicester are to qualify once more for Europe. Bosancic, who had replaced the ineffective Tinkler for Barnsley, provided an unnecessary sprig of excitement when he twice fouled Zagorakis and was sent off five minutes before full-time.

Afterwards, Wilson implored that no-one asked him the obvious. 'Don't anyone dare ask me how I feel,' he said. He was asked, instead, how his players felt. Since we had seen several break down in tears on the pitch, we already knew the answer. 'Their confidence is very low at the moment. They are absolutely gutted to have their Premiership place taken away from them. They are very disappointed. Some of them are spewing back there,' said Wilson.

While he spoke, laughter and chatter rang out from an adjoining hospitality room. Glasses were being clinked, greetings exchanged. The constant hum of merriment was irritating and disrespectful. In one room, a wake of sorts, in another, a party of sorts. 'People will have sympathy with us for about two minutes, but that will be it.' said Wilson.

The Premiership party will continue without Barnsley, though their neat, flamboyant football, the romance they provided, and their sheer valour will linger for much longer than Wilson predicts.

---

*Friday 8 May 1998*

Danny Wilson vowed to stay at Oakwell. 'I remain totally committed to the club, the chairman, and his directors. My aim is to confound all the critics again and lead the Reds back into the top flight next season,' he said.

His hallowed status among Barnsley fans had remained steadfastly intact. A letter by supporter Barry Thompson in the *Barnsley Chronicle* illustrated the depth of feeling: 'What a man. His courage, dignity, his humility and his pride are all the things we in Yorkshire hold dear to our hearts. God bless you, Danny, for all you have given us. We really appreciate it.'

---

LAST ORDERS AT OAKWELL BUT NO CALL FOR BITTER
*(The Times, Saturday 9 May 1998)*

Another drink, please. No problem, says the barman. He is unhurried, able to break off and tell his young assistant that the crisps are in the back, love, near the crate of Becks.

Where we might expect sullen demands for beer, more beer, with a chaser of gin and bitter – so very bitter – lemon, a slick of well-mannered, well-sober people request shandies, orange juice and, just occasionally, a bottle of beer; 'Just the one, mind, I'm driving.' Barnsley, just a day earlier, had been relegated from the Premiership. The annual function of the Barnsley Supporters' Club should form the epicentre of the town's grief. 'It's like a Golden Wedding in here,' says the man near the bar who has a joke for everyone. The remark is apt, for proceedings do have the genteel, dignified, china cups a-chinking air of a golden wedding. Also, everyone in the room, is, for better or worse, married to Barnsley FC.

John Dennis is asked to say a few words and he saunters between the tables, past the vol-au-vents and serviettes, to the far end of the room. 'I don't think there are many chairmen of a team just relegated who would be made to feel so at home among supporters,' he begins. His speech is short, he indicates that he is still hurting from the shock of relegation; it will be a few weeks yet before his arid sense of humour returns.

As he walks back to his position at the bar, head hung low, it is impossible to remain untouched by the warm heart that still beats within this football club. There is no clamour for retribution, no complaining, but merely a sanguine acceptance that everyone – the manager, the players, the directors, the supporters – gave their best, and there was nothing greater they could give.

There was a pact among them that they would kick and scream against the dying light of a Premiership life, but, simultaneously, there was a fierce determination that the season was a special gift, something to be relished in itself. This is not to say that they do not want more of it; for Barnsley, the sequel is already at the planning stage.

Most of the Supporters' Club committee have followed Barnsley from the early Sixties. They were at Oakwell in April 1973 to see Mick Butler score the only goal of the game against Exeter City when the attendance was a mere 1,428. They can remember frightful FA Cup defeats by Rhyl in 1970 and Marine in 1975. These are supporters who have seen former rivals like Bradford Park Avenue, Workington Town, Barrow, Newport

County, Southport and Aldershot slip into obscurity or oblivion. Relegation from the country's top division has to be placed into the context of this legacy.

The supporters' committee – a retired prison officer, a solicitor, a bank manager (the Yorkshire Bank, of course), and a salesman – agree to pick through the bones of Barnsley's season. Where, just a few years ago, such a meeting might have taken place in a damp caravan propped above the puddles by bricks, we are among the padded seats and carpets of an executive box. Oakwell is in darkness beyond the glass panel, but it is possible to make out the impressive Ora Stand rising to our left. The infrastructure of Barnsley will remain regardless of their league status.

Why has the club flourished in a town where hope and dreams were presumed extinct alongside the coal industry? 'There have been two catalysts,' said Alan Bloore, chairman. 'The first was Allan Clarke coming here as manager in 1978 and the other was the appointment of John Dennis in 1989. They have both been part of building the club up to what it is now.' Dennis, a fruit and vegetable merchant, is popular with supporters, viewed almost universally as 'one of them'. 'A few years ago we asked John if the supporters could have a seat on the board. He said to me, "What the hell do you think I am?"' said Bloore. The Supporters' Club accepted the point. The request was withdrawn.

Gary Willard, the hapless referee who sent off three Barnsley players in their 3-2 defeat against Liverpool in March, is blamed for, at the very least, unsettling the team. It is noteworthy that before that infamous game they had won four of their previous five matches, yet since then they have won just one out of seven. The bitterness has now largely subsided, but the Supporters' Club is campaigning to investigate the wider principle of referees and their accountability.

Danny Wilson's future plans have understandably provoked much speculation. 'He is at the turning point. It would be very courageous if he stayed with the club now because if he went he would go out as a god, and stay a god for life as far as Barnsley fans are concerned,' said Ray Brammer, the treasurer. Bloore suddenly recalled a remark Wilson made at a meeting earlier in the season. 'He told us that he has never broken a contract in his life, and he is under contract here. I think he'll see it as a failure if he gives up on us now,' he said.

Manchester United visit Oakwell tomorrow and their supporters travelling across the Pennines will witness a celebration rather than a wake. The official Barnsley chaplain, the Rev Peter Amos, will leave at half-time to prepare for his six-day walk to Birmingham where he is due to present a petition to the G8 summit. The Barnsley players and staff have all signed the petition calling on the world's richest nations to wipe out debts owed by Third World countries. They gave their signatures during the most fraught weeks in the club's history; Barnsley, clearly, has maintained its perspective.

---

*Sunday 10 May 1998*

### Barnsley 0 Manchester United 2

Manchester United, still smarting after missing out on the championship to Arsenal, played several of their younger players but still outplayed Barnsley. Andy Cole and Teddy Sheringham scored their goals.

---

COLE SPOILS TOBY'S RELEGATION PARTY
*(match report, The Times, Monday 11 May 1998)*

The big lad wearing No 49 appeared to be set for a place on the substitutes' bench at least. He had impressed in the warm-up, only taking a breather to chat with Alex Ferguson, the Manchester United manager. Lamentably, in a match filled with new faces, we were denied the first appearance of Toby Tyke, the impish Barnsley mascot, but it was a close call; it was that kind of afternoon.

Barnsley were determined to leave the Premiership in style and laid on a rousing relegation party. The Supporters' Club had pinned up the sign 'We're Coming Back' across the office window, just in case anyone had any doubts. The press corps were handed strawberries when they collected their passes.

United had no truck with sentimentality and took the lead just minutes after the kick-off. Sheringham floated a telling cross to Cole who turned sharply to drive it beyond Watson. The passion that has epitomised Barnsley's season was in evidence as Ward and Hristov went close, but United's greater finesse was visible in flashes. As the rains came down the visiting fans left their uncovered seats in droves long before the end and many missed Sheringham's exquisitely taken goal.

The Barnsley supporters sang in the rain, many taking off their shirts in defiance of the elements and United's superiority. Adie Moses came closest to finishing proceedings with a goal for the home side, but May fended it from the goal-line.

The unfamiliar faces in United shirts performed well, Brown especially, though where they will be in the queue for a first-team place next season is open to question.

For their part, Barnsley return to the Nationwide League with a great deal of applause ringing in their ears, though they will need to acquire a sharpness of thought and deftness of touch that United, championship runners-up or not, exemplify. Danny Wilson said that a lack of experience had been his team's downfall this season. 'You cannot rely entirely on young lads,' he said. 'They have done marvellously well, but they have had dips in form.'

He paid tribute to the supporters, who had remained loyal despite relegation. 'They have enjoyed themselves and really made the most of our season in the Premiership,' he said. 'They have been a breath of fresh air.'

After the final whistle, Toby Tyke reappeared to perform a Full Monty routine and the crowd sang 'You'll Never Walk Alone'. There was not a dry eye in the house.

---

# A WAKE OF SORTS

## Tuesday 12 May 1998

Ashley Ward pledged his immediate future to the club, though doubts remained over out-of-contract players Clint Marcelle, Arjan de Zeeuw and Jovo Bosancic. Neil Redfearn intimated that, as he would be 33 at the start of the forthcoming season, he would consider a move to a Premiership club. Georgi Hristov's future in English football would depend on whether he was granted an extension to his work permit.

---

## Friday 14 May 1998

Readers of *The Sun* voted Neil Redfearn as their 'Unsung Hero' of the season. 'I genuinely find it flattering that so many people think so much about me,' he said. He polled 43 per cent of the votes, with Sammy McIlroy, the Macclesfield Town manager, the runner-up. Arsène Wenger, the Arsenal double-winning manager, was voted best manager by a huge majority, though Danny Wilson was runner-up; further evidence of his popular support.

*The Sun*'s award was proof that Redfearn had established himself on a national level more than any other Barnsley player. David Watson had earned notice for some dogged displays, but he was still seen widely as a novice, a player for the future. Ashley Ward, meanwhile, was the clear favourite among the Oakwell crowd. This suggested a certain blasé attitude to Redfearn's habitually solid performances. He had been a model of consistency for seven seasons, after joining the club in September 1991.

Much of Redfearn's renown came by virtue of his inclusion in thousands of 'Fantasy League' teams throughout the country. His excellent goalscoring record and regular appearances saw him accrue scores of points. He missed just one match, the 4-1 defeat at Southampton, when he was suffering from a heavy cold. His tally of 10 goals made him the highest scoring midfield player in the Premiership, albeit that three were via the penalty spot.

Statistics produced by Carling Opta at the end of the season showed Redfearn was the team's most consistent player. The squad was assessed by computer for shooting, passing, crossing, tackling, clearances, and dribbling. Redfearn, with 930 points, scored over 100 points more than his nearest rival, Ales Krizan. He had 114 shots in the season, almost double Ward's total, in second place.

Aside from the technological testimony, Redfearn was perceived as archetypal Barnsley. He toiled valiantly, played for the good of the team, tackled hard but fairly, rarely moaned, and, just as importantly, he had the fabled appearance of a tyke – broad-shouldered, rugged (he suffered a broken nose in a match at the age of 17), a no-nonsense haircut and a no-nonsense approach.

Noticeably, when Redfearn's form dipped at the end of the season, the team lost confidence around him. His lack of pace was suddenly manifest amid the scurry, and opponents were forewarned of his tendency to shoot given a yard of space between the centre circle and their penalty area. He was closed down immediately and rarely had the pace to race past a challenge or the ingenuity to side-step it. During the last 20 league matches he scored just two goals from open play.

_____

### RAIN OR SHINE, ROGUE ELEMENT MAKE THEIR MARK
*(The Times, Saturday 16 May 1998)*

August, beautiful sunshine. The first day of the new football season. Heat so intense it hurts to grip the car steering wheel. A St John's ambulanceman, neat but over-wrapped in his uniform, trails through Barnsley town centre, presumably on his way to Oakwell. He passes a throng of pink-skinned men huddled around a pub entrance, beer in their hands, beer in their bellies.

'Hey you,' they shout to this man twice their age and half their size. 'Who the fuck do you think you are?' He scurries away, pretends not to hear.

# A WAKE OF SORTS

May, cold wind, driving rain. The last day of the football season. A steward carefully watches a group of supporters. It would be gracious to call them excitable, but execrable would be more appropriate. They are out of their seats, out of their minds. They bray, swear, growl and gesture at their Manchester United counterparts. Finally, the ringleader is hauled from the mob. He makes a few token shoves, but soon surrenders. After a few paces he abruptly – and cowardly, considering the steward is off-guard – headbutts him in the face. Where we might expect the sound of a collective wince from the crowd, or a sigh, or even a few shouts of 'steady on', there is a cheer, a hearty, pathetic cheer.

Strange folk, Barnsley folk. Nowt as queer. They have been portrayed as cheery, clappy, happy Northerners, but among their number are racists, bigots and thugs. There are also, in far greater quantities, some of the most decent, warm-hearted people in football. No half-measures, then.

The final match of a long, fascinating season revealed the best and worst of Barnsley. After losing to Manchester United, the supporters sang out an emotional rendition of 'You'll Never Walk Alone'. The players and manager returned to undertake a lap of honour. Beforehand, fans had been asked repeatedly to keep off the pitch. It was a language they did not understand. Stewards were flattened, police officers pushed roughly aside; sentimentality had given way quickly to hostility.

The players were lost in the brutal throng, scurrying desperately to safety. Ashley Ward, their player of the season, was ambushed and lifted on to shoulders. He looked like a man about to die, thrashing around amid this reckless flesh, bruised by their adulation. It made for an undignified exit, a truly Barnsley end, a not-quite-right end.

The talk throughout Barnsley is of an immediate return to the Premiership. Sometimes, this stubborn, immovable belief in the team, the town even, is unpleasant. The humour drops from faces, there is a vague threat, an unnecessarily sinister air. It's only a game, lads, nothing personal.

Barnsley, in truth, will struggle to return at the first attempt.

They have played poorly for several weeks and recorded just one win in the last nine matches of the season. Their celebrated passing football has not been evident for some time and there is not enough pace and precision.

Danny Wilson needs to augment the team with at least three players, and they need to be playmakers, for he is already top-heavy with heart and endeavour. In Barnsley, Wilson is beyond criticism, a celestial being in a tracksuit. There has been little focus on his managerial stock, and much on his doughty what-a-bloody-nice-blokeness. This has meant that his failings have had more than a touch of thick, non-drip gloss.

Three of his close-season signings from abroad, namely Hristov, Tinkler and Krizan, were speculative and, by Barnsley's standards, expensive at £2.6 million in total. They added much to the wage bill, and little to the team. The home buys, meanwhile, Barnard and Ward, were unquestionably good business, both playing nearly 40 games each and rarely off-form.

At the start of the season Wilson's tactics were naive. It took him too long to realise that his players were not as good as he thought. When he insisted that they curtail the flicks and dribbles and play, instead, neat six-yard passes, the pastings stopped.

In the relegation run-in he consistently chose a front two of Fjortoft and Ward. They might be useful as battering rams (with, in Ward's case, some skill), but they were bulls for the slaughter in the top division where a striker needs greater finesse.

Wilson has pledged himself to Barnsley for at least another season. Though this news has received little notice, it is an extraordinary gambit. 'He could leave here a god now,' said one supporter recently. Indeed, he would depart on surprisingly good terms, maybe to one of a clutch of big-name clubs where fans are bleating that they have underachieved, which means, in some cases, that they have not won the championship.

If Barnsley are outside the promotion frame next season, Wilson's allure to top clubs will diminish significantly. They are slaves to whimsy and the team that Wilson built will be dismissed as a one-season wonder. His decision to remain loyal to Barnsley is both praiseworthy and daring; time will tell whether it is foolhardy or not.

The personality to watch at Oakwell, perhaps more so than Wilson, is the club chairman, John Dennis. For Wilson and his players, Barnsley is a football club, a job, but for Dennis it is a life in itself. He is pugnacious and canny, on fire with ambition. The momentum that has driven the club from obscurity is from him, allied to a united board of directors.

They are backed by a commendable team largely hidden from public view: Michael Spinks, the workaholic general manager; boot-room grafters like Eric Winstanley, Colin Walker, Peter Shirtliff and Norman Rimmington; and the youth development team led by Peter Casken and Maurice Firth. The supporters too are essential, the thousands upon thousands that do not confuse passion with aggression.

In all likelihood, Barnsley may take a few seasons before they return to the Premiership, but the blend of expertise and good sense, married to a fiercely idiosyncratic nature, will ensure that their good heart beats on, and on.

---

*Monday 18 May 1998*

Ron Atkinson, the Sheffield Wednesday manager, was told that his contract would not be renewed for the forthcoming season. Dave Bassett, who had just led Nottingham Forest to the Nationwide League Division One championship was named as favourite to succeed him. Howard Wilkinson, the FA's Technical Director, and Danny Wilson were the other names linked with the position.

---

*Tuesday 19 May 1998*

Apart from writing about Barnsley, I found myself talking a great deal about them during the course of the season. I was asked a thousand times (at least) whether I thought they would survive in the Premiership, and the next question was invariably: 'What do you think of Danny Wilson?' It was a difficult question to answer, at least in a few words.

The season over, there was, finally, some time to reflect. John Dennis asked whether I had enjoyed viewing the club from close quarters. 'Yes, apart from my fall-out with Danny Wilson,' I said. 'I heard about that,' he responded. 'I'll have a word with him.'

I was grateful for his suggestion, but decided to contact Wilson personally, and offer an explicit olive branch. I did not want our disagreement to remain like a mortar bomb thrown among so many words of compassion. I had grown very fond of Barnsley, and there had been times when my loyalty to my own club had been tested rigorously. During the Easter Monday game against Newcastle, for instance, I had to turn off the radio commentary, such was my nervousness. I tuned in towards the end, and when Shearer scored I switched it off again, this time in temper. Rochdale, meanwhile, who were guaranteed safety from relegation because of Doncaster's plight, had lost 3-0 at Swansea. I hardly gave them a moment's thought.

At the end of the Leicester match, when relegation was confirmed, I stayed in my seat to witness the Barnsley supporters singing their devotion for a good 15 minutes after the final whistle. Most of the other reporters had left the stand. Jon West, the journalist who had covered the club intensively for the *Sheffield/Barnsley Star*, walked to the front of the press area and stopped in his tracks. He looked pale, but was at least able to speak as I approached. 'They're unbelievable, aren't they?' I could only nod, the lump in my throat too big to swallow.

I regretted that I had not made contact with the Supporters' Club earlier in the season, for these are real football people – knowledgeable, friendly, helpful, and loyal to the cause, without being sycophantic. While I had referred to the hostile element of Barnsley's support, I had too often neglected to mention these compassionate, sociable fans who were far more valuable to the lifeblood of Barnsley FC.

In the circumstances, it was a shame to leave Oakwell with any kind of unfinished business. A newspaper article is ephemeral, while a book has a certain amount of longevity. A meeting with Wilson would take a couple of hours, and, perhaps, provide a congenial closing note:

Dear Danny

The columns that formed my 'Life At The Top' articles in *The Times* are to be gathered together over the next few weeks and compiled in a book of the same name (with additional words) to be published by Queen Anne Press.

We haven't spoken since January when you were curt with me on the phone. My letters of apology did not solicit a response, so I'm not sure where we stand. I think it would be a shame if the book is written/published against this background of vague animosity, especially since, otherwise, my season in the company of Barnsley was so enjoyable.

If we were to have one last meeting/interview it would make a fine closing chapter, though, out of the necessity of deadlines, it would have to be at some point over the next two weeks.

Best wishes
Mark Hodkinson

---

### Thursday 21 May 1998

Jayne Kilner, Wilson's secretary, called and said he would be available for interview, but not until he returned from holiday in the middle of June.

---

### Sunday 24 May 1998

The Premiership received its 'new Barnsley' when Charlton Athletic beat Sunderland at Wembley in a thrilling Division One play-off final. The media tried to instil the same romance into Charlton's elevation, but it was not quite the same. They had played in the top flight many times before and did not emanate from a forgotten town in provincial England. The other teams promoted to the Premiership were Nottingham Forest and Middlesbrough.

---

*Friday 22 May 1998*

Barnsley announced that season tickets would remain at the same price for the forthcoming season. This amounted to a per-game reduction because there were an additional four home fixtures in the Nationwide League.

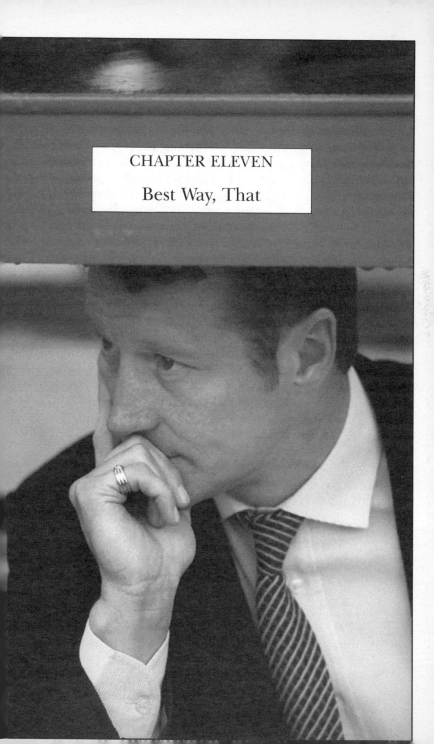

# CHAPTER ELEVEN

## Best Way, That

*Saturday 30 May 1998*

Eric Winstanley, first team coach, was taken ill while at Oakwell and driven to Barnsley District General Hospital by Roy Hatton, the head groundsman. He had suffered a mild heart attack and was transferred to Sheffield's Hallamshire Hospital. 'I went to see him and he was looking and feeling well. He is already talking about the new season,' said John Dennis. As a player, Barnsley-born Winstanley appeared in almost 500 league and cup games for the first team during an 11-year spell. He returned later to join the coaching staff, initially working with the junior players.

---

*Monday 1 June 1998*

Eric Tinkler was informed by Philippe Troussier, the South Africa coach, that he had not been selected for the country's World Cup squad. He would have been the first Barnsley player to take part in the World Cup Finals.

---

*Tuesday 9 June 1998*

Jayne Kilner phoned and asked me to confirm that I still wanted to interview Danny Wilson on Monday 15 June. I told her I did.

---

*Friday 12 June 1998*

Ora Electronics UK Ltd, the club's sponsors, extended their deal until the year 2000. 'The fee remains confidential but I can safely say it is a substantial six-figure sum,' said Michael Spinks. Barnsley announced that season-ticket sales had exceeded 5,000 and they expected to sell 10,000 before the end of the summer.

*Monday 15 June 1998*

I phoned the club before I left home and was told that everything was fine for the interview. It was the day when England were due to play Tunisia in their first match of the 1998 World Cup. There had been fighting between rival fans the previous day in Marseilles, the venue for the game, and radio bulletins were gorging on the news. I was about 30 minutes from Barnsley when I received a call on my mobile phone:

'I've got some bad news for you, I'm really sorry about this,' said the voice.

The interview was postponed because 'Danny is playing golf this morning, something to do with Terry Yorath's son.' I guessed that it was a charity tournament in honour of Danny Yorath, the son of the former Wales international and manager, who had died of a heart condition at the age of 15. Jayne Kilner said Wilson would phone me himself later in the week and rearrange the interview.

———————

*Wednesday 17 June 1998*

I called the club and explained that the publishers had already extended the deadline and would be unable to do so again if the interview did not take place soon. Wilson was contacted by the club at home and agreed to see me on Friday 19 June at 10 am.

———————

*Thursday 18 June 1998*

The fixtures for the forthcoming season were announced. Barnsley's season would begin with a home fixture against West Bromwich Albion on Saturday 8 August, followed by games against Crewe Alexandra and Stockport County. Supporters believed the omens were good because the promotion season also started with a fixture against West Brom.

Work permits were renewed for Ales Krizan and Clint Marcelle. Georgi Hristov had already learned that he would be able to stay with the club for another season at least.

---

*Friday 19 June 1998*

Dressed in a light, flowery dress, the young mother stuck to her task doggedly. The reception area at Barnsley was flushed with light, the summer finally here.

'Does he need boots to be a mascot?' she asked in a strong South Yorkshire accent. Boots sounded more like 'boats'.

Jayne Kilner on reception was doing her utmost to remain polite and responsive, despite the constant bleeping of the switchboard. The toddler at his mother's feet was dressed immaculately, white curls framing a sweet, cherubic face. After his début on the pitch at Oakwell, a career awaited in television adverts.

'Can I sit here, mummy?' So polite. He was helped on to the chair by his mother who did not look down. She was craning her neck, attempting to converse through a small glass panel open just a few tantalising inches. Welcome to Barnsley, welcome to a stiff neck.

'Can he just wear normal socks? The ones that go with his kit bury him,' she said. Jayne did not really know the answer, but three lights were flashing, three lines ringing, so she nodded sympathetically.

Out on the car park, trucks whisked by and men in ties with rolled-up shirt sleeves stared intently into theodolites. While they worked, children arrived on bicycles. They propped them up against a wall and took turns to stand guard while they went into the club shop. Inside, last season's Premiership T-shirts were marked down at just £5 each.

Jayne caught sight of me over the woman's shoulder and shouted: 'Danny isn't here yet, do you want to pop back in a bit?' I walked out to the car park. The sun had turned Barnsley orange and sent light dancing all around. People walked languidly from their cars to the shop or the ticket office. The cold sweat of a season just gone and a season to come seemed inconsequential. In fact, under the warm sun, nothing seemed to matter a great deal. I returned to the reception a few minutes later.

'He's just arrived,' she said.

I could hear my heart beat. This was it, the showdown, the match of the season: Wilson v Hodkinson. I walked along Grove Street towards the players' entrance. The mobile phone fastened to my belt felt like a pistol. I had to squint in the sun. Townsfolk were at their gates, watching the stranger passing by. The dust swirled. No-one would get out of here alive, and Ennio Morricone had already written the soundtrack.

The corridors under the West Stand were deserted. The board-room door was open and, as Jayne had requested, I entered. It was cool in there, untouched by the sun. It was a long, windowless room panelled in wood, and at the far end were two rows of cushioned benches facing each other. The door opened suddenly and I rose instinctively, ready for Round One. It was Norman Rimmington, the club's kit man and a veritable Uncle Barnsley.

'Is this where Danny's doing the interview?' he said. I moved towards him. I was about to ask if he remembered me from our meeting just a few months earlier. He turned and left before I could speak, on the hunt for tea and biscuits, or perhaps a sponge and bucket; he had the rugged, been-there-done-it look of a boxing corner man.

Finally, Danny Wilson entered. He looked like he had just returned from a yachting holiday. Big smile, caramel tan, cotton slacks. We were shaking hands before we knew it. My nerves were disarmed by his bonhomie. I remembered the warm and friendly man of our first meeting, not the fury on the phone.

The moment did not seem right, so nothing was mentioned. We talked instead about his team's Premiership season. He rued the poor start, the lack of players with experience at the top level, the suspensions, the reverence they had shown to teams. He was matter-of-fact, never moaning, or whining. Gary

Willard had 'lost the plot' in the Liverpool match, but he was not to blame for Barnsley's relegation. 'It was not down to one particular game. I suppose, in the end, it was down to finance. We wanted three more players. Ashley Ward was one of them, but we never found the other two,' he said.

I had heard the explanations before, on local radio interviews, on television, in his weekly column in the *Barnsley Chronicle*. His answers were straightforward and ostensibly candid, but were avenues, always looping back to the beginning, and never branching off into new areas. His eyes bled honesty, but the words were parched, kept in check by a meticulous, astute mind. No matter the question, and their covert journalistic wile, we were back to a stock answer, something that sounded familiar.

Wilson was proud of his antecedence in the game, his 22 years in professional football. He was a supremely intelligent man, someone who had walked through life and appropriated wisdom from all quarters. He had learned to watch his front, and his back, to sense the metaphorical sliding tackle. On coaches travelling to matches, dressing rooms at half-time, the players' lounge after full-time, the training pitch on a misty Monday morning, he had met them all – the chancers, the posers, the wasters, the creeps, the greedy, the arrogant, the stupid. Football had granted him access to all life-forms, and he remembered every one, vividly.

The media, like players and supporters, directors and office staff, was part of the job, something else to deal with. Since he brought a bloody-minded professionalism to all aspects of his life, so he played journalists with sweet perfection. No doubt he remembered the man from the *Bury Times* (Bury were his first Football League club) or the occasional misquote in the 'Pink Final' (the Saturday football paper published by the *Manchester Evening News*). He had learned to be polite, direct, and even crack a joke or two. There was, though, a line drawn, a no man's land. He realised that journalists were people to whom their first loyalty was 'the story' and that a careless word was combustible. Wilson's heedfulness and discretion was well hidden.

Sometimes, it was parallel to exemplary diplomacy. We discussed briefly his plans for the future. He said he was ambitious, and finished: 'Of course, I'm like any other football manager, I would love the chance to manage (he paused here, very briefly) England or Barcelona.' He purposely did not name a top English club, but lifted his aim higher, to ensure he missed any target from which speculation could take a foot-hold. Where, in others, one might have detected an undercurrent of circumspection or faced a litany of surly no-comments, with Wilson there was always a smile, a dimple part-way down his face to counter-balance the keen eyes. It was impossible to dislike him, so much strength of personality garnished with charm and humour.

An hour had passed. It would have been easy to pretend nothing had come between us. I owed it to myself. Once more, I was trying to tempt him away from his mental safety rope, asking him to analyse his own personality; the usual do-you-see-the-boy-in-the-man gush. A phrase, a corny one at that, came into my head.

'You're a tough cookie, aren't you?'

He shrugged his shoulders, this was my chance.

'Well, you told me where to get off, didn't you?' I put down my notebook. There was no change in his expression, no sign of nervousness. He might have been reading from an invisible card.

'As I saw it ... ' he started. He had seen it as I knew he had seen it. He thought I had been disloyal back in January, but, either way, the telephone conversation had been the end of the matter. What was all the fuss about? We were grown men. There was mutual respect; that was why we were in the same room together.

'I don't bear grudges,' he said. 'We both said our piece on the phone and that was it as far as I was concerned.'

He should have replied to my letters, returned my phone calls, I said. He did not apologise, but intimated that, since my access to Oakwell had not been affected, by implication no animosity had remained.

The notebook was not picked up again. Wilson noticed, and

became much more open. We discussed the personnel at the club. He could have been anyone talking about his job of work. He liked some colleagues, disliked others; so-and-so was 'greedy'; someone else was trustworthy, another wasn't. A friendship, the real thing, that is, would be something to covet with Danny Wilson. He was passionate, opinionated, ready with a quip ('I'm uncomfortable with all this fame and adulation. Before this, I think I was just seen by most people as a little twat!'), and, one imagined, fiercely loyal.

We needed a photograph of Wilson for the cover of the book. As we walked outside on to the street, he revealed that he had come into 'work' solely to do the interview. He apologised for postponing our original appointment. He had unexpectedly been given an early tee-off time at the golf tournament and had to leave much earlier than expected.

The photographer had a specific shot in mind. He positioned Wilson in the shade alongside the wall flanking Grove Street and the West Stand. He was to walk towards the camera, looking in a certain direction. A few people gathered to watch, workmen who had been painting inside the ground and residents leaning on their front gates in the sunshine. Wilson broke off occasionally to share some banter. He was asked to walk the same few steps several times. In his summer gear, it looked as if he was modelling. He was a little bit shy of the attention, uneasy at having to take this same stroll again and again. There was, however, no mutter of complaint, he did it with good heart, patient and compliant. Eric Winstanley, looking a little thinner after his heart attack, was spotted in the background, potentially 'spoiling' the shot. 'Hey Eric, clear off will you,' shouted Wilson affectionately.

The session finally over, Wilson was waylaid by a passing supporter offering some advice on tactics for the forthcoming season. We had to shout our goodbyes from a distance, and were immediately stopped ourselves by a few of the painters.

'What did he tell you? Has he signed any more foreign lads?'

'He's told us nothing, he doesn't give much away,' I said.

'Best way, that,' one responded, laughing.

On the drive away from Oakwell, I took a wrong turn and was caught in the one-way system in the town centre. It seemed pre-determined that I was to have one last look at Barnsley. The new replica shirts had obviously reached the club shops, for they were everywhere. The man selling copies of *Socialist Worker* outside the college had one, so did the teenage girl sitting on a wall by the Town Hall; I saw scores in the space of just a few hundred yards. Ten years ago, there would have been just a handful. All seemed well in Barnsley but the season was to bring one final twist.

---

### Wednesday 24 June 1998

The FA announced that it was to take no action against Barnsley for the pitch invasions during the league match against Liverpool at Oakwell. The FA statement read: 'We are satisfied that Barnsley FC discharged their responsibilities with all due diligence.'

---

### Thursday 25 June 1998

Neil Redfearn left Barnsley and signed for Charlton Athletic for £1 million. 'I did not want Neil to go, but there was no way I would deny him the opportunity to remain in the Premiership,' said Danny Wilson. Redfearn had made 335 league and cup appearances for Barnsley and scored 83 goals.

---

### Monday July 6 1998

Barnsley contacted several media organisations and informed them of a news conference to take place at Oakwell at 1pm. There had been speculation in the weekend newspapers that Danny Wilson was to leave the club and take over at Sheffield Wednesday.

By mid-morning, radio reports were announcing that the conference would be to make public Wilson's departure, and his succession by John Hendrie. Meanwhile, another press conference was due to take place at Hillsborough at 3pm, where Sheffield Wednesday would reveal their new manager as Danny Wilson.

---

SHEER SPONTANEITY OF DENNIS HELPS TO EASE OAKWELL PAIN
*(The Times, Tuesday 7 July 1998)*

The media was the easy bit, and John Dennis knew as much. Even while the Barnsley chairman spoke into cameras and tape recorders, supporters were wandering off the streets into Oakwell. Danny Wilson, their manager of four seasons, had departed, just a week after the exit of club captain, Neil Redfearn. Suddenly, Barnsley, the Athletico Dreamsville of modern football had started to look like F.C Ordinary.

Oakwell is a place where fans flock just to watch training sessions, so when news is spreading that Wilson is leaving, to join local rivals Sheffield Wednesday, a pilgrimage is soon under way. Dennis did not side-step the fans, nor the issues, when he was waylaid at the edge of the pitch. 'In the end, Danny had a hankering to go to Sheffield Wednesday, and it was as simple as that,' he said. Granted an unexpected audience with the chairman, most supporters could only articulate their shock, and little reason. A flat cap or two were realigned after much head-scratching. Babies held in tattooed arms cried in the sunshine.

It would be impossible for outsiders to understand the depth of affection that Barnsley people hold for Wilson. His departure will feel like a death in the family. One supporter was moved recently to write in the Barnsley Chronicle: 'What a man. His courage, dignity, his humility and his pride are all the things we in Yorkshire hold dear to our hearts. God bless you, Danny, for all the things you have given us.' The letter was penned after relegation from the FA Carling Premiership.

Wilson had pledged himself to Barnsley and pointed out on several occasions that he had never, on his own instigation, broken a contract during a 22-year career in the professional game. He will presumably now argue that his move was a club-to-club agreement, for which Barnsley will receive an undisclosed sum of compensation. 'We did all we could to make Danny stay,' said Dennis.

Once the shock has subsided, there is every likelihood that it will be superseded by hostility. Almost 12,000 season tickets have been sold for the forthcoming season. Fans will suggest that a 'deal' with Sheffield Wednesday had been in place for some time but delayed while Wilson issued duplicitous rallying calls to the Barnsley faithful.

'This story is already circulating locally but it is a complete and total fabrication,' said Dennis. 'It has all taken place very quickly in the last two or three days.' Dennis, understandably, is reluctant to concede that the departure marks Barnsley,s return to football's hinterland: 'I said to the players that one man has left this football club. This is a strong, proud, determined club and because one person has left, it does not change our ambitions and ability to make further progress.'

While Dennis skilfully appeased the fans, John Hendrie, Wilson's successor, was sitting in the stand conducting numerous radio interviews. ' We should not linger in the past, this is the future now,' said Dennis, pointing upwards to Hendrie. The appointment is a masterful tactical move, for Hendrie is another messiah-in-waiting in Barnsley. Like Wilson, he is adored, for his passion on the field and his good humour and humility off it. He will become the club's player-manager, on a three-year contract.

He returned from a family holiday in Spain on Saturday and was contacted immediately by Dennis and asked to replace Wilson. 'It was a bolt out of the blue. I had no inclination at all. It was a surprise, a nice surprise. I am going to give this my best shot and I believe this club will go from strength to strength,' he said.

As the throng of supporters saw the familiar burly figure of John Dennis in front of them, and a former player of the season sitting behind, ready to become their new player-manager, Oakwell did not seem quite the foreign place they had expected. 'Hey John, do you accept season tickets with sellotape all over them?' asked one smiling fan. 'Why?' asked the chairman. 'Because I ripped mine up this morning but I'm thinking of sticking it back together.'

---

### Thursday 9 July 1998

At any other club, it would have been very different, but Barnsley is unique. It invests a great deal in certain people, perhaps more than it should. Their affection, once it is earned, is fanatical and borders on the sentimental: 'I bloody well, bloody love you, I do.' Danny Wilson, more than any single person before, was revered in the town. Politicians, cricket umpires and television personalities had nothing on him. They fell for his charm, his cheeky, chirpy guile, a charisma that could transcend boyishness to coarse, adult bloody-mindedness. Here, they found Barnsley in human form: gritty, unfancied, determined, efficient, a small man prepared to meet the big world head-on.

During Barnsley's season in the Premiership, the nation fell in love with Wilson, but the admiration was qualified, always tinged by a sprig of realism. Football management was governed by a revolving door, and the time between entry and exit was – in most cases – rarely more than a couple of years. There was an acceptance that Wilson, like all the rest, would eventually succumb to the lure of a bigger club with its armoury of prestige, wealth, and sheer footballing tradition.

In Barnsley, with commendable ingenuousness, they thought it was for ever. It felt like a gang, where they had all spilled blood and sworn an immortal allegiance. They granted Wilson a near-mythical status, a god amongst men. He was above the temptation of money and status, the beautiful maverick in a world of whimsy and avarice.

There had been talk of Wilson moving to Sheffield

Wednesday for nearly three years, and it had intensified during the 1997-98 season, when David Pleat and, later, Ron Atkinson, were sacked – any other term would be inappropriately delicate for a club with famously bullish tendencies. In the end, it seemed too obvious that Wilson should choose Sheffield Wednesday.

While he appeared candid on some subjects, Wilson was extremely guarded in response to gossip linking him with other clubs. 'I've got a job to do here,' he would retort. He was interviewed on Radio Five Live immediately after the memorable win at Anfield and was asked about managing Sheffield Wednesday. For once, he was flustered. 'I don't think you should be asking me questions like that at a time like this,' he said. The interviewer tried again, and was rebuffed once more. I was listening on a coach with the euphoric Barnsley supporters. A few seconds after the interview, one piped up: 'He didn't say he didn't want to go to Wednesday, did he?' No one responded.

The move was, in many ways, understandable even to the most partisan Barnsley supporters. He had previously played for Sheffield Wednesday; it was undeniably a bigger club; his wages would be significantly higher (reportedly £1.5 million over three years), and, very much to his credit, he had left Barnsley in an infinitely better state than he found it. His actual departure, however, was a personal PR disaster, and it left many Barnsley fans extremely hurt. A banner appeared at Oakwell overnight reading: 'Johnny [John Hendrie] Is Jesus, Danny Is Judas.' It was a raw, angry sentiment, but, across the town, it was generally shared, in various diluted forms.

Keith Lodge of the *Barnsley Chronicle* was the man at the front-line of supporters' emotions and he estimated that 95% of telephone calls and letters sent to the paper had been critical of Wilson. 'He got some flak. They were using words like Judas, betrayal, and saying good riddance to him.' The anger had stemmed both from Wilson's behaviour after the end of the season and the timing of his announcement.

He had not given any indication that he would leave

Oakwell, in fact the opposite. 'As far as I am concerned I am going to be here next season. We have a big challenge ahead of us,' he told the Barnsley Star in a piece beneath the headline: '"I Won,t Walk Out" – Wilson.' Similar articles appeared in other local papers. Wilson was aware that they contained overt pledges of loyalty, but he did not complain that they were inaccurate or hint, however vaguely, of a possible departure. Football fans understood the code, and Wilson could have used the appropriate phrases to prepare fans for the disappointment. Neil Redfearn, for example, had subtly made it known that he might leave the club, and stated his reasons (which were largely accepted) for several weeks before joining Charlton.

Understandably, supporters were uplifted by Wilson's initial loyalty and it was a major factor in rallying support within the town. His often-repeated promise that he had 'never broken a contract' was passed around like a precious stone. On the day he left almost 12,000 season tickets had been sold. The man who had asked for allegiance and strength in adversity had suddenly left the fold. To compound matters, he had joined local rivals and, just a few miles down the A61, he was already singing another song. He told journalists that he did not mind being Wednesday's third or fourth choice as manager [several, including Walter Smith who joined Everton instead, had turned down the job], such was his desire to move to Hillsborough. He talked as if Wednesday were the love of his life, a calling above all others. Barnsley fans checked the record books: he had spent three seasons with Wednesday and played 98 league matches.

Conspiracy theories spread out-of-control through Barnsley. Some suggested that Wilson and the club were in cahoots; the tacit agreement was to announce the move only after a significant number of season tickets had been sold. And was it not suspicious that Wilson had not signed a single player for Barnsley during the summer? And why had John Hendrie not been selected to play towards the end of the season – was he already in preparation for a behind-the-scenes role?

John Hendrie was the ultimate appeasement to the Barnsley supporters. He would receive their complete backing, and much of their adoration for Wilson would be refocused, though a shard of caution would temper their commitment. Their trust would never be total again. There was no edifice with Hendrie, he was a good-natured, trustworthy man. Insiders felt his back-up team of Eric Winstanley and Peter Shirtliff would 'nurse' him into management, where decisions had to be made quickly and without sentiment.

For my part, I found Hendrie unusually friendly and trusting for a professional footballer. In the course of setting up one interview with him, he rang and spoke to my girlfriend. She thought he was Irish at first, and he played the offended Scotsman for a good five minutes, before leaving her laughing and slightly embarrassed. When I did the piece with his wife, Linda, about the life of a footballer's wife, I stayed at their home until nearly midnight. Their son, Joe, passed around tacos which he had coated with a mountain of cheese and tinned tomatoes. It was a pleasure to share their company, and easy to feel at home.

At the beginning of the 1997-98 season Barnsley fans would have been distraught to learn that, less than a year later, their club would be relegated and that their manager and captain would no longer be at Oakwell. When they look into the eyes of the two Johns, Dennis and Hendrie, that now form the figurehead of the club, they see, however, an integrity, determination, and honesty that they see in themselves.

## FIRST TEAM APPEARANCES AND GOALS  1997-98

| | League | FA Cup | Coca Cola Cup | Total | Goals |
|---|---|---|---|---|---|
| Appleby, Matty | 13 (2) | 1 (1) | 1 | 15 (3) | 0 |
| Barnard, Darren | 34 (2) | 5 | 3 | 42 (2) | 4 |
| Bosancic, Jovo | 13 (5) | 3 (1) | 0 | 16 (6) | 2 |
| Bullock, Martin | 24 (10) | 3 (2) | 1 (1) | 28 (13) | 0 |
| Eaden, Nicky | 33 (3) | 5 | 2 | 40 (3) | 0 |
| Fjortoft, Jan Aage | 13 (2) | 0 | 0 | 13 (2) | 6 |
| Hendrie, John | 7 (13) | 4 | 0 | 11 (13) | 3 |
| Hristov, Georgi | 11 (12) | 1 (1) | 1 (2) | 13 (15) | 5 |
| Jones, Scott | 13 | 1 | 0 | 14 | 3 |
| Krizan, Ales | 10 | 1 | 3 | 14 | 0 |
| Leese, Lars | 8 (1) | 0 | 2 | 10 (1) | 0 |
| Liddell, Andy | 13 (12) | 1 (4) | 2 | 16 (16) | 4 |
| Marcelle, Clint | 10 (11) | 3 (1) | 0 (2) | 13 (14) | 0 |
| Markstedt, Peter | 6 (1) | 1 | 0 | 7 (1) | 0 |
| Morgan, Chris | 10 | 3 | 0 | 13 | 0 |
| Moses, Adrian | 33 (3) | 6 | 2 | 41 (3) | 0 |
| Redfearn, Neil | 38 | 6 | 3 | 47 | 14 |
| Sheridan, Darren | 20 (6) | 3 (1) | 3 | 26 (7) | 1 |
| Shirtliff, Peter | 4 | 0 | 1 | 5 | 0 |
| Tinkler, Eric | 22 (4) | 2 | 2 | 26 (4) | 2 |
| Ten Heuvel, Laurens | 0 (2) | 0 | 0 (1) | 0 (3) | 0 |
| Thompson, Neil | 3 | 0 | 1 | 4 | 0 |
| Ward, Ashley | 28 (1) | 6 | 3 | 37 (1) | 10 |
| Watson, David | 31 | 6 | 1 | 38 | 0 |
| Wilkinson, Paul | 3 (1) | 0 | 0 | 3 (1) | 0 |
| de Zeeuw, Arjan | 27 | 5 | 2 | 34 | 0 |

## FA PREMIER LEAGUE
### Final Table, 1997-98

|                      | P  | W  | D  | L  | F  | A  | P  |
|----------------------|----|----|----|----|----|----|----|
| Arsenal              | 38 | 23 | 9  | 6  | 68 | 33 | 78 |
| Manchester United    | 38 | 23 | 8  | 7  | 73 | 26 | 77 |
| Liverpool            | 38 | 18 | 11 | 9  | 68 | 42 | 65 |
| Chelsea              | 38 | 20 | 3  | 15 | 71 | 43 | 63 |
| Leeds United         | 38 | 17 | 8  | 13 | 57 | 46 | 59 |
| Blackburn Rovers     | 38 | 16 | 10 | 12 | 57 | 52 | 58 |
| Aston Villa          | 38 | 17 | 6  | 15 | 49 | 48 | 57 |
| West Ham United      | 38 | 16 | 8  | 14 | 56 | 57 | 56 |
| Derby County         | 38 | 16 | 7  | 15 | 52 | 49 | 55 |
| Leicester City       | 38 | 13 | 14 | 11 | 51 | 41 | 53 |
| Coventry City        | 38 | 12 | 16 | 10 | 46 | 44 | 52 |
| Southampton          | 38 | 14 | 6  | 18 | 50 | 55 | 48 |
| Newcastle United     | 38 | 11 | 11 | 16 | 35 | 44 | 44 |
| Tottenham Hotspur    | 38 | 11 | 11 | 16 | 44 | 56 | 44 |
| Wimbledon            | 38 | 10 | 14 | 14 | 34 | 46 | 44 |
| Sheffield Wednesday  | 38 | 12 | 8  | 18 | 52 | 67 | 44 |
| Everton              | 38 | 9  | 13 | 16 | 41 | 56 | 40 |
| Bolton Wanderers     | 38 | 9  | 13 | 16 | 41 | 61 | 40 |
| Barnsley             | 38 | 10 | 5  | 23 | 37 | 82 | 35 |
| Crystal Palace       | 38 | 8  | 9  | 21 | 37 | 71 | 33 |

Suggested further reading:
*Weekend In Dinlock* by Clancy Sigal (Penguin)
*Barnsley: A Study In Football 1953-59* by Ian Alister and
Andrew Ward (Crowberry)
*A Kestrel For A Knave* and *The Price of Coal* by Barry Hines
(Penguin)
*Only A Game?* by Eamon Dunphy (Penguin)
*This Sporting Life* by David Storey (Penguin)